"I Follow the Course, Come What May"

"I Follow the Course, Come What May": Major General Daniel E. Sickles, USA

Jeanne W. Knoop

Jeanne W. Knoop

for Martha

July 22, 2000

Signed at Gettysburg, PA

VANTAGE PRESS
New York

FIRST EDITION

Published by Vantage Press, Inc.
516 West 34th Street, New York, New York 10001

Manufactured in the United States of America
ISBN: 0-533-12607-X

Library of Congress Catalog Card No.: 97-91251

0 9 8 7 6 5 4 3 2 1

To the memory of Daniel Edgar Sickles, for his inspiration to me to rethink his long life from a different point of view.

With my compliments, Sir. . . . .

I have said to you before that I do not deem it a wise course nor recommend it to any friend: it is mine and I will follow it come what may.

—Daniel E. Sickles

Contents

Preface

Daniel Edgar Sickles has always been written about by men in the past. I do not know if they have been easier or harder in writing his life story, but perhaps a different look from a woman's point of view is now due.

It is my intention to find this enigmatic and complex man not only as a soldier, but as a husband, lover, friend, father, and grandfather to the men and women in his long life. I hope that I may find him objectively and without slanted emotionalism.

Maybe there are judgments and suppositions made by me here that are incorrect, but who really knows?

Words are all that we have to chronicle interpretations we see.

He chose not to write his story himself, although I believe that he may have wanted to give his side of the stories circulated. There were many newspaper editors and book reviewers who would have had "a field day" with the contents.

Another thought would be that he did not "give a damn" what other people thought; it was his life.

It seems that whatever he did or said, he was considered to be a power hungry, ruthless man, or worse. He knew that anyone crippled by a fear hastens the very thing he fears.

"The Washington Tragedy" roamed the entire world in 1859 and he fed the flames, making his wife write her own "death sentence." So much better to have kept quiet. Many plans must have had to be abandoned now, that they could not be part of his future past this point.

Some people seemed to put the worst possible slant on his actions after that portion of his life, and that made for even more controversy. He was damned if he did, and damned if he did not.

There were no loving relationships, no real moral purpose behind Dan. He certainly had a lot to remember and reflect upon as he approached the last decades of his life.

No one truly knows what he thought about or how his life turned out to him. I still would treasure such an autobiography that I could have made my own judgments. But it was too big a name, too hard a story, and too many enemies in at least almost six different lifetimes in ninety-four years. He realized that if we live in fear of death, we shall come to our death not having lived. He knew it all anyway, on his terms, but what a grand story it would have been.

What a charming devil! The best and worst of the nineteenth century.

A lifetime friend or a vilifying opponent. He was all of this and more.

His name will always live on and be spoken of by those who know the entire story.

Books have been carefully read, and from them occasional bits of comment, adventures, and criticism have been woven into the story; a character study of this complicated man.

Acknowledgments

For assistance on doing research for this book, I wish to thank, in particular, two Daniel Sickles decendants, John Shaud, and James William Davidson, for their patience and understanding and providing me with so much of Sickles's family history, not found elsewhere, including little known facts pertaining to his long life and many careers.

I also wish to thank the friends at the Summit [New Jersey] Library Reference Desk for their invaluable help with the microfilm repository and the hundreds of Inter-Library volumes that I have been loaned for the many years spent on research. Their support was most appreciated.

I give special thanks to Cynthia Sullivan, a good friend, who also took on the character of Dan Sickles as she read the story and lent me a very skilled hand in guiding the manuscript from my written work onto the software necessary for the completion of the book.

And last, but certainly not least, I bestow on my husband, William, my many thanks for his help, supporting me throughout the years of constant work that I gave this project and proofreading for many hours, putting aside his own books to be read, as is his greatest joy. Without his understanding of why this new approach to understanding Dan Sickles was of so much importance to me, my task would have been harder.

"I Follow the Course, Come What May"

One

July 2, 1863, the Day the World Changed

Dan Sickles sat on his horse, Tammany, surrounded by his aides, watching the progress and reversals of the fighting on the lands near his headquarters on the Trostle Farm. He had ridden back and forth all through out the day. The farm was about a quarter of a mile north of the wheatfield. He was on a vantage point observing at about 6:30 P.M., when he was hit by a solid-shot, twelve-pound cannonball, which tore almost through his right leg and left it dangling below the knee.[1]

It was a freak wounding, for the shot had hit the rider so slightly that it did not spook the horse, which had been slightly wounded already, and it remained under control. His aides helped him as he almost fell from the horse, guiding his leg over the saddle and lifting him down. They carried the wounded general to the outside wall of the large barn. He remained conscious and composed and was concerned about the possibility of being captured, so requested that he be placed beside a large boulder on the side of the barn. He took a sip from a small flask of brandy, and wanted a cigar. An aide took one from the cigar case, bit off the end, lighted it and gave it to Sickles, who puffed away.

This senior aide, Major Henry Tremain, who had just returned to the site, was terribly upset, seeing the man for whom real affection had increased since their days on the Peninsula Campaign. Pale and obviously in great pain, Sickles exclaimed excitedly, "Quick, quick, get something to tie it up, before I bleed to death." A leather strap was found for the task, but it did little good. He then ordered his command turned over to Major General David Bell Birney, Third Corps Division commander. To stop any rumor of his death, which would demoralize his troops, he kept smoking the cigar and waving to his men. An ambulance arrived soon after dusk and General Sickles was transported to one of the Third Corps hospitals. Sickles lay on a makeshift operating table, surrounded by the surgeon and his assistants. The only light was from candles held in the sockets of bayonets. The Reverend Joseph Twichell, the Third Corps chaplain, and one of the general's best friends, administered the chloroform and remarked that General Sickles's bearing and words were of the noblest character. He said, "If I die, let me die on the field. God bless our noble cause."[2]

The Third Corps hospital was about three miles away on a farm belonging to one Daniel Shaffer. Within one hour Dan Sickles had been given the choice of two surgeons to perform the amputation of his right leg. One, Dr. J.T. Calhoun was the assistant surgeon, Third Corps medical director, Second Division. The other surgeon was Dr. Thomas Sim, U.S. Volunteers, Third Corps medical director, Second Division. Sickles chose Dr. Calhoun.[3]

There was no sleep for the general that night, the severely damaged leg having been removed. General Sickles was asked if he wanted anything to drink. He asked if there was a bottle of champagne available. Although none could be found, a warm bottle of white wine was. Dan requested that the bottle be put down the well to be chilled, and this was done for him. After cooling, it was brought back to him and he drank some, then asked that it be returned to the well for recooling.

This trip to the well and back to the general went on all night, until the bottle was empty. The next day he was taken by stretcher to the small town of Littlestown, Pennsylvania, where a railroad link existed. The town of Gettysburg, of course, had another station, but it was considered too dangerous to use at that time, and in addition was being used to capacity by the wounded of the last two days. The stretcher was placed across the backs of two train seats, and he rode thusly, along with fifteen hundred wounded Federal troops who could be transported out of Gettysburg.

Dan arrived in Washington on Sunday, still never off the stretcher, three days after the wounding, with Dr. Sim, Major Tremain, Lt. Col. James Rusling, and the two aides still with him. It was on this trip from Gettysburg to Washington that Dan Sickles learned about the defeat of Pickett's Charge, launched by the Confederates on July 3rd.

When the train arrived in Washington, there was great jubilation all around about the victory at Gettysburg. Dan was very weak after the wounding and the train ride, which must have been uncomfortable, trying to maintain some sort of balance on a moving train lying across two seats, one in front of the other.

Following the removal of the lower leg, Dr. Calhoun did not place it with other severed limbs in a basket as usual, to be buried in Gettysburg with thousands of others. Somehow Dr. Calhoun showed Dan a year-old flyer requesting exhibits for the new medical museum that was to be started in Washington, and Dan agreed to contributing the leg bone for this purpose. Dan asked that it be placed in a small box, after wrapping well and perhaps in some ice, if found, and the limb with or without the attached foot

Major General Daniel E. Sickles

went back on the same train as the general. The first museum was either located at the Smithsonian Castle, or at Ford's Theatre, being at both sites for a time.

Dr. Sim and the aides stayed with Dan, as the wound was still considered mortal and few men lived after such amputations during the war. The crisis time was approaching, and sterile techniques were not known or practiced, so Dr. Sim kept Dan on the same stretcher for days, even afraid of moving him onto a bed. This must have been very uncomfortable with his being still in great pain and shock. Through it all, Dan managed to shave himself, as he had always done and would always do each day, no matter what happened.

Although there were to be no visitors that Sunday in Washington, Tad Lincoln, the president's son, made his way into the room followed by the president, who had come to visit his good friend of many years. On their first meeting in 1861, Dan had come to Washington to beg Lincoln to allow Federal volunteers to be able to enter the army in addition to the state volunteers. If the cause was union, as mentioned, then at least some of the troops should be federal, which was only right by Dan's thinking. This was allowed after awhile, the war enlarging the need for different troops.

The president asked about Gettysburg and they talked at length about the three days' happenings. Sickles was happiest to see him above all persons. Dan related that his wound was possibly mortal, and the president said that he had many plans for him and he was needed for these plans.

If any words could lift Sickles's spirits, these were the ones he needed to hear. Smoking a cigar, he and the president talked a long while, the general being sharp but still wincing in pain. As the day was very hot in Washington, and he called his valet, Mosely, whom he had employed for some time, to pour cool water over the stump. The president arrived the next day as well to sit and visit and give support to his friend.[4]

It is interesting to have learned that President Lincoln ordered tanbark put down on F Street in front of the house where Sickles had rooms, to cushion the many traffic noises for the general's benefit.

This thoughtful gesture must have helped during a trying time.[5]

The most often told story about Lincoln emanated from General Sickles, the colorful commander of Meade's Third Corps, who lost a leg at Gettysburg. When Lincoln visited the convalescent in Washington three days after the battle, the president admitted to the general of some alarm during the battle. In fact, though he would not wish it to be known, he went into his room, locked the door, and got down on his knees to pray to GOD for victory. "I told HIM this was HIS country, and our war was HIS war, and that we could not stand another Fredericksburg or Chancellorsville, and then and there I made a solemn vow that if HE would stand by our boys at Gettysburg, I would stand by HIM. And although He was not a "meeting man," Lincoln continued to Sickles, "somehow or other sweet comfort crept into my soul that GOD ALMIGHTY had taken the whole business up into HIS hands and that things would come out alright for Gettysburg."[6]

Sickles rested and worried a lot, especially when rumors circulated that General Meade was considering breaking up the Third Corps, and putting the remaining units in other corps. The Third Corps men were unhappy about this, but could do nothing about it. Sickles kept in touch with General Birney and other Third Corps officers about the command. He was straining at the bit and writing to everyone whom he thought could influence on any decisions to be made. He felt alone and, out of touch, and unable to do much about it. No visits to expedite the proposed plans were possible. He was not able to travel, but his mind was overactive to get back to command. He wrote Edwin Stanton for another command, possibly in Texas. Dan had known this man since his trial for murder, and Stanton had won acquittal for him and was a friend. In fact when Sickles's only son was born, he was named George Stanton Sickles, as an honor to this man. All through the son's life, he was known as Stanton Sickles.

No contact with anyone was able to change the situation in which he found himself, and this was new and frustrating to Dan Sickles.

Dan loved the Third Corps with all of his heart, as he had built it up from the earliest days, and General Meade would not break it up! He also wrote Edwin Stanton about his old friend, Charles K. Graham, who was captured at Gettysburg and was a brigade commander under Sickles most of the war. He was being held in a Richmond, Virginia, prison and Sickles wished him to be exchanged before he became too ill from the life there if possible. This was done and Dan was most pleased about how it turned out.

Dan fretted and stewed and healed in that order. His leg was still painful and could not be fitted with an artificial leg that had become available then at the time, until the stump was sufficiently healed and returned to normal size.

Dan was most happy to have progressed well enough to call on President Lincoln on crutches, which he mastered fast and well. Agile he had always been. He bade a fond farewell and was helped by the aides upon a train from Washington to Jersey City, New Jersey, where he switched from the railroad to a launch fitted out with a multitude of good friends, who were there to welcome their friend back from the war with loving good cheer and to add to that the fine fancy luncheon sailing over the Hudson River up to Ninety-First Street and Bloomingdale. This small hamlet was on the river, a veritable paradise of lawns, outbuildings, with a fine house and farm, and a dock for boating. There to meet Dan was Teresa, Laura, his wife and daughter. What a reunion for them. That must have been a heartfelt meeting for Dan to see them after so long, and for them both to see him after his wounding. A strange meeting for the hero of Gettysburg. More of that later.

Dan stayed at his home in Bloomingdale until August 11th, when the heat, even along the Hudson River, was too much for him. He and his two aides went by train to the Fort William Henry Hotel on Lake George, New York, located in the Adirondack Mountains. He now had his two aides, Captain Moore and Captain Fry to accompany him. They were to lift the crippled man about when traveling.

What a change from the wartorn lands they had been on. Poor food and all of the hardships even for officers. From that to living in a luxury hotel filled in summer with wealthy guests mostly from New York City, who were bug-eyed when seeing General Sickles almost directly from the battlefields of Gettysburg! Only in the papers had they of any hint of war news, so to have so important a participant in their own hotel was an exciting experience. He made a sensation being there and his arrival was the most important happening all summer. There was no porch-sitting for him. . . . He played billiards, went hunting, shot deer, fished every day, moving about with ease on his crutches. The hotel gave a grand soirée in his honor. He lamented the fact that there would be no dancing with the beautiful women there with whom he would have enjoyed the dancing that had been so pleasurable before, all of his adult life.

Major General Daniel E. Sickles, age 44, at the time of the Battle of Gettysburg.

A man who has lost a limb knows that one who has shall never be the same man, and he knew that well.[7]

Not one to get too far down for long, he enjoyed the time there as well as his aides did. He was not an easy man to spend the most of every twenty-four hours with, but the aides were living high as well. They loved him and were pleased to see him active again after being inactive for months. It was time for them all to enjoy the scene after so many years on the fields of war.

The general left the resort on September 17th for New York. He was refreshed and healed somewhat better and headed toward as much as he could of his old life, under new circumstances.

Most harsh opinions of Dan Sickles were softened as time went on. He was feted by the Third Corps whose men had, with love, contributed and presented him, by way of General Birney, with a fine barouche carriage drawn by four matched horses. As he climbed into the carriage with General Birney, the ovation was spontaneous and with much loud cheering. His men wanted him back in command, missing a leg or not.[8]

So ends, "July 2, 1863, The Day the World Changed." Forty-four years, almost half a life lived. Now, how to make a fulfilling future, for it would turn out to be another fifty years!

Two
Searching for an Education

Daniel Edgar Sickles was born on October 20, 1819, in New York City. He was the son of George Garrett Sickles and his wife, Susan Marsh Sickles. Right off there is some dispute about the date of his birth. His quote, at some point in his life, is of having been born in 1825. Mention has been made that his parents were not married until later in the year 1820 and that he may have felt shamed by this uncertainty. However, I believe, that as a politician, being thought of as five years younger on the record, once said publicly, would stand until it appeared to be the truth. This may not be true, but family papers attest to the 1819 date. The same change is done today, and will always be done by politicians and many thousands of other citizens.

George Garrett Sickles was born in the year 1800 in Maugerville, New Brunswick, Canada. The family could have at one point been considered Tories and removed themselves, as many Tories did before them during the early days of the Revolutionary War, returning later on, as many Loyalists were doing in the same century. He had learned the printing trade during his youth, which was to figure prominently in the Sickles family future.

New York City was a growing, bustling city of over 150,000 people, looking for a living, and living quarters for thriving businesses. George Sickles was at the right place at the right time with plans for success in real estate investments. He was considered to be the first patent attorney, somewhat a politician, and an opportunist whose fortune flowed and ebbed from near poverty to financial success.

His son, Daniel, was as strong-willed and headstrong as his father before him. Both of his parents were proud of his ability and friendliness, but worried by his lack of subordination to authority. This became evident in his fifteenth year in 1836, when he was enrolled at the Glen Falls Academy for young gentlemen in upstate New York.

At this time, a typhus epidemic was raging in the city of New York, and his parents thought that the move to the country would be wise and might make "a man" of their son, with someone else making the effort instead of themselves.

While a student there, he used to spend any free time in the back room of *The Messenger,* the local Glen Falls newspaper. He was given a job as a printer's helper, at the bottom rung of the ladder. He caught on quickly to the ways of typesetting and even some reporting. He found that he liked the life, and the learning of words that were to come so easily to him all through his life.

Troubles came to him at the academy when the strict headmaster was to whip him for insubordination, but found himself being whipped. This was the end of the academy. Dan would not accept the punishment and that day ran away from the school. He went back to *The Messenger,* resumed work there for eighteen months, and learned journalism.

When Dan's parents brought him back to New York from Glen Falls, they sought new plans for his future, as the ones they had chosen had not worked out to anyone's benefit. Dan was still running away and had to have focus placed on what course of action would get him at last, "on track."

George Sickles owned land in what is now Livingston, New Jersey, a rather large farm that stretched from a small settlement, later known as Morehousetown, all the way to the Passaic River toward Chatham, New Jersey. The area was settled by German families over a large portion of Essex County, consisting of Roseland, known then as Centerville, Caldwell, Essex Fells, and Livingston, known in earliest times as Canoe Brook.[1]

The George Sickles home still stands on Beaufort Avenue, known earlier as Little Neck Road, and Featherbed Lane. It has been greatly changed since the 1830s, but still the outlines of the Federal era New Jersey farmhouse can be seen. It is a large house set on lovely, well-tended gardens and lawns, albeit less land lies behind the house, and now a major highway cuts off the area where the farmlands stood then.

The Passaic River was lovely in the 1830s, with drinkable water, large trees, and grassy areas. Part of the river was used for boating, with rented gondolas for parties and church picnics. Also a good-sized brook ran through the Sickles land to the river.

George Morehouse was a Civil War veteran who lived on Beaufort Avenue where the Livingston traffic circle joins Route 10. When Mr. Morehouse died and the traffic circle was built, some of the earliest homes were torn down. Old barns, quaintness, and beauty were lost forever. Now Eisenhower Parkway runs along, cutting off the area with highway and cement, and a large mall, recently combined to make a wasteland of a once beautiful spot.

His parents' plan was to settle Dan on the farm to learn the business of a gentleman farmer, and to teach him by a "hands on" policy to employ the latest farming techniques in the 1830s. There were cattle in some number and forage crops, such as meadow hay, which Dan would learn to manage. The problem was that Dan did not like the farm life, as it was entirely too quiet and lonely for him. He was not to be a farmer, and it is remarkable that he spent as long as one year trying it out. At age eighteen, he had other plans for himself. One late summer day, he packed a few belongings and walked away a long way to Princeton, New Jersey, where he hoped to enter Princeton University in the fall term. He finally did arrive there on foot after the long walk, and learned in an interview with a college official, that he did not have enough money to enroll. He was disheartened, but not for long! He headed straight for the local printing shop to find work. What he had learned previously and liked, would now sustain him. He had learned that at least.[2]

His father finally learned where he was and tried unsuccessfully to get him to return. Dan refused, and would not consider returning until his father agreed to let him enter another local college, New York University, to commence his education.

In time, George Sickles sold the Livingston farm to a man named Hoffman, and the land passed to his son and his heirs after that.[3] George then built another fine farmhouse in New Rochelle, New York, where he lived, in addition to a New York City address, and had his lucrative law practice, even into advanced age.

I might add the following interesting comment here from the Livingston Historical Society's brochure on local history: "Daniel E. Sickles was the most important person to live in Livingston from a historical point of view."[4]

Around this time, George Sickles's investments soured and he found it difficult to help him financially, so Dan took a job as a typesetter on Fulton Street in New York City. He would wait and see just when he would enter college.

Before long, his father's assets improved dramatically again and Dan was allowed to start his education as originally planned. His father had to plan carefully to see that his son would be tutored for long enough to make up for the lost time since leaving Glen Falls. He and his wife realized that a third party was needed, a keystone, to keep their son interested and under control, which seemed to be lacking in their home, but could such a person be found?

George Sickles had a friend named Da Ponte, who lived on Spring Street in New York City. The family would have been called Bohemians in that day. They were well educated, musically driven, intellectually superior, and a possible good choice. The youngest of the three Da Ponte sons was Lorenzo, a professor at New York University.

This would be the answer to the Sickles prayers for Dan's education. The family did not have a lot of money, and there were many mouths to feed. They lived in a large, at one time, fine house, now run down, but there was much laughter, with loving ties in the group. There was also good food, wine, and a stimulation that would encourage Dan. The move was arranged, and a new life opened at last for this intelligent young man. The head of the family was Lorenzo Da Ponte, who spoke seven languages; his wife, Signora Da Ponte; two unmarried sons, Joseph and Lorenzo; and Charles, who had a wife and a two-year-old son, Durant.

In his old age, the father, Lorenzo, had for some reason adopted, from Croton Falls, New York, a fourteen-year-old girl, who it is possible, may have been his blood daughter, by the name of Maria or Eliza Cooke. All lived in the Da Ponte home.

Lorenzo senior had had a very interesting life. He was a Venetian Jew who had turned to Catholicism and become a priest. He was the librettist for three of Mozart's operas, *Le Nozze di Figaro, Cosi Fan Tutti,* and *Don Giovanni.* He was also a close friend of the rake Casanova and the Court Poet of the Emperor Joseph of Hapsburg.

A musician by the name of Antonio Bagioli came from Italy and stayed with the Da Pontes. He soon was taken with the lovely young lady who had been adopted. They were married, and lived at the Da Ponte home. Somehow there would always be enough room and food even for an extra person to join the family.

In not too long a time, a baby, whom they named Teresa was born to the Bagiolis. She was the little darling of the family, a cuddly beauty even at a young age, being born in 1835. Here in this outgoing environment Dan lived and continued to learn. He must have enjoyed all the interplay in the family, being the lonely single child of his parents. He was frustrated at times when the family lapsed into the French language, then Italian, then Spanish, then German. Dan wanted to know it all! They decided that their house guest and pupil would learn faster the languages spoken if they spoke no or little English before him. The house was a mad one, but the plan worked and Dan became almost fluent and his pleasure increased knowing what they were saying to him and each other. His quick mind absorbed all that he heard and his pleasure increased. There was talk of opera and fine classical music, and more worlds were to open for Daniel Sickles.

Lorenzo, the son, was thirty years old and was America's first professor of the philosophy of history that he taught at New York University. Dan's imagination was captured by him and the two became fast friends. Dan was ready for entrance to the university after tutoring by Lorenzo.

By now, Lorenzo senior, was well along in his life, and he died after living ninety years. His last act was to compose an ode called "Farewell to Life." He died the next day.

Dan's mentor, Lorenzo, who suffered from intestinal tuberculosis, caught pneumonia and died in 1840. This was Dan's first great loss, devastating him, and he grieved and suffered great mental anguish. The funeral was filled with Dan's emotional outbursts and lamenting cries. After that there was no returning to college. In 1840, Dan entered the law offices of Benjamin F. Butler, who had been Attorney General under President Van Buren. In 1843 he was admitted to the bar. It is interesting to note that his father spent two years tutoring his son, even though Dan did not live with his parents, but boarded in a home in Bowling Green until he moved farther up Broadway and only a little more than a block from the Bagiolis' home. The Bagiolis had left the Da Ponte home after the death of Lorenzo, the elder.

Dan opened his own law offices and was developing a reputation for some questionable practices, which were gaining some notoriety among local lawyers. He was accused of having "too much" zeal. He made money and a lot of friends. As the saying goes—A wise man knows everything, a shrewd one, everybody!

Dan had also, during this time, become interested in politics and joined the Tammany Hall group of Democrats. Tammany was a tough and scrapping organization of men, who like George, his father, made things happen. Dan also had some questionable friends, who roamed New York City after dark, seeking feminine company and sometimes trouble. He probably, at this time, became acquainted with a beautiful prostitute named Fanny White, whom Dan wanted to be his mistress only. The cost of such an arrangement was high because of her lodgings and all of the accouterments attached to her living. They spent much time together and got along well. This liaison continued intermittently for over five years.

Three
Growing Up with Teresa

While Dan was forging ahead in business, Teresa Bagioli was a child, and becoming more beguiling each year. She was like a little sister to him, teasing and delighting his vanity. As time went on, she took pleasure in conversing in one language and then switching to another, and back again. Dan was always welcome at the Bagiolis' home and spent as much time as he could find to be with her. She was, almost part of his family because he had never really had any siblings. The two of them would take long walks, go berrying, look for bird's nests, attend the circus, and go to the river to see the ships in the harbor. They both had a love of nature, and the adventures of the new and wonderful world of New York City.

When Teresa was twelve and Dan was about twenty-eight, she requested a horse to ride, asking would he please get one for her. Dan found a gentle mare, and she took to the saddle like a wild child, never having ridden before. He had been riding for years since his farm days, but this new challenge opened an entire new world for Teresa. He would scold her for going too fast, too soon, but he forgot that was the way he had learned to ride also. Even then, she was a creature of moods as he was also. They truly shared their lives together. It was a pleasure for him to leave the strenuous legal battles and political brawling to spend time with this charming girl who grew more beautiful, blossoming into her early Italian mature heritage.

Teresa had never had a beau, being a schoolgirl at the Manhattanville Convent of the Sacred Heart in New York City for many years. She was now fourteen, and before Dan knew it, fifteen. She was by now a voluptuous little beauty, with shiny black hair, flashing dark eyes, and an angelic smile. She only had eyes for Dan, however, and continued to use seduction as she only imagined it to be whenever he was near. Dan noticed, as did other men who saw her, and was intrigued by her beauty. He felt a male pride to be seen with her, and could feel that this relationship was becoming more to him than friendship. How long before a sudden change would take place, that neither of them could seem to control?

Dan Sickles's effect on women of all ages was a positive attraction, and he was used to giving back the same to the women he met. Women, young and older, single or married, saw something in Dan and responded to this. A look from those gray eyes, which seemed to see so far ahead, but smiled like a caress, brought the ladies to him like a magnet. He had this effect on most women nearly all of his long life. This was always a diversion from his role in public life, but never, I feel, as important to him personally as getting along with other men in the army or in politics. For some men, loving family relationships head the list of life's happiest moments and accomplishments, but with Dan it was not as important as his day-to-day life as a man bound for success, wherever and with whom it took him.

The time just hinted at, came to them both, and new problems and adjustments soon would arrive for a future life together before they were aware of it. Teresa became pregnant. Both sets of parents were opposed to the union.

Teresa Bagioli Sickles, probably taken at the time of her marriage to Daniel Sickles at age 17. She was believed to have been photographed by Mathew Brady in both New York City and Washington, though the origin of this photograph could not be confirmed.

An early photograph of Daniel E. Sickles, at about the age of 33. After the author contacted numerous sources, the origins of this photograph are still unknown.

The difference in age and the knowledge that Dan had had a life containing many other women for years, had led them to believe that it would not lead to happiness. Dan listened, but decided that marriage was the best solution, and a wedding day was announced. They were married on September 27, 1852.[1]

They were clearly infatuated and perhaps truly and deeply in love, and a quick decision was the proper one. Teresa was sixteen and Dan almost thirty-three. Teresa was delirious with happiness. She had, at last, her dear, dear Dan to herself, although she knew too little of this man with whom she would try to share a life. She knew his nature as tempestuous, while other people saw her as a child. But if you read her letters to him, there is more woman in her words than child. She would try to give him so much of her love, that he would need only her and their child to come, to make him happy and true only to her.

Teresa probably conceived in the summer of 1852, before the civil ceremony at which the mayor of New York City, Ambrose C. Kingsland, officiated on September 27, 1852. Six months later they were married again in a Catholic ceremony in March 1853, in the private offices and residence of Archbishop John Hughes. Teresa must have been obviously pregnant for the last ceremony, but her parents must have requested official church sanction, a religious rite.

The couple went to live with her parents, the Bagiolis, at 92 Prince Street in New York City. Her parents wished to be near their daughter for the delivery in a few months' time.

Four

Tammany Life; Fast and Loose

Dan made friends easily, and they were rich and poor alike. The city's leading financiers, the quiet, the loud, all seemed to know, and most to admire him. Many of these friends continued to be there for him all of his life. Once a friend was made, he was kept, and even some enemies became good friends as time went on. One was Emanuel Hart, a surveyor and fellow Tammany member, as were many of them. John L. Graham, a lawyer, Thomas F. Meagher, an Irish revolutionary who had escaped going to a British penal colony, and who was also a lawyer and an editor. This friend was later to become a Federal Civil War general as leader of "The Irish Brigade." Henry Wikoff, the "Chevalier," who was to cause much trouble with his too free mouth and his meddling. Dan, an Episcopalian, made many friends of both Jews and Catholics.

Dan was always in need of more money, although he made enough perhaps, but it was never enough to cover his debts. He chose to live high on fine-tailored clothes, gambling, the best foods and wine, brandy and cigars, in addition to keeping Fanny White in the same style.

New York City grew steadily, approaching three quarters of a million inhabitants. The immigrants from Europe flooded Manhattan, and nine out of ten stayed there once they had arrived in port. Mainly they were Irish and German, and the Democratic party courted the vast numbers seeing that eventually they could easily sway votes to their candidates.

Dan loved to sit and drink with friends at Delmonico's where they could discuss business, politics, and the theater. He had a magnetism, wit, and intelligence, and could speak knowledgeably of just about everything. He noticed the effect this had on his friends and acquaintances and was soon in private, conjuring up future scenes of higher political aspirations, even perhaps, a race for the White House. Most all politicians someday dream of this, and it did not seem out of the question for him!

Dan borrowed money as such as he often lent it to friends. He was considered loyal and possessing a great depth of sentimentality. I believe that Dan valued camaraderie above all else in life. Although there were many women in his life, his friends counted for more in the long run. Dan's parents were continually upset by his actions and financial losses, but his letters to them were respectful and border on affection. Money was to be spent, not saved, was his motto. More could be obtained from somewhere. . . . .

In 1847 Dan ran for public office, and was elected State Assemblyman. Word of his alliance with Fanny White became public knowledge when he even took her up to Albany to show her the vast assembly rooms. She was known, and her visit caused much concern. Dan was censured for allowing and arranging for the visit.[1]

Dan joined the New York State National Guard as a private in the Twelfth New York Regiment. He took to the task like a new West Pointer, reading all of the many books on tactics that the soon-to-be officers in their third year read. He studied hard and worked long hours at the books. He found that he liked this knowledge, and finally advanced to a colonel of the guard. When a West Pointer graduated, he was a second lieutenant and would not have received instruction as to how to command men. This was not taught. This would prove a liability for officers in the field later on at the beginning of the Civil War. It had to be learned AFTER graduation, in the service, wherever the officer arrived for duty.

In Tammany meetings, Dan was able to talk with conviction and belief, and be charming, no weakling, however, and he took to learning self-defense and carrying a pistol and knife as some of the others were known to have done also. He made even more enemies, but he could stand up for himself anyway.

Dan was always immaculately dressed, caring about the way he looked and presenting himself always at his best. Things were going well, and according to plan. Through his Tammany connections, he became a committee chief and was able to implement many decisions that helped Tammany and himself. A plum was offered to him in 1853, when he was made Corporation Counsel for New York City, and he kept the position for eight months.

While in that position, Dan saw a need for a park that would rival those of the chief cities in Europe. A large park was needed as the city grew, and the sight chosen was small and not conveniently located. He persuaded the City Council to appropriate seven hundred acres, and it was to be called, Central Park. The area was in bad shape to begin with. Masses of rocks and boulders, and even swamps. No trees at all that could be saved. When he left for London and a position at the American Legation, the plans sat dormant until his return two years later.

When Dan returned to New York City, the Central Park plan was brought up again and went on to be completed as soon as possible. Dan got his friend, John Graham's brother, Charles, who was an engineer, to design a proper park for the city. It was to be laid out with miles of macadamized roads, bridges, bridle paths and countless trees. Tons of soil were brought in for fill and grooming around the boulders and trees, and there was before long, a park to be proud of. History seems to have lost this moment, sad to say, as mention of Dan's dream is unobserved, although the park is now truly beautiful and worthy of his pride. He has been referred to as "The Father of Central Park."[2]

It might be added that Charles K. Graham was a lifelong friend of Sickles, becoming his brigade commander of the Third Corps during the Civil War.

Five

The Secretary of the American Legation

Dan Sickles went to Washington to see President Franklin Pierce, with whom he enjoyed a friendship, seeking to help gather for his friend, August Belmont, a diplomatic appointment overseas. His star was rising faster now with his still occasional law practice, his Tammany Committee work, and his plans as Corporation Counsel of the City of New York. At a busy Democratic gathering in New York in May, Dan ran into his friend, John W. Forney, who asked him if he would be interested in a position as Secretary of the American Legation in London.

The Minister of the Legation was to be James Buchanan. The salary was a mere $2500 a year. Dan laughed and remarked that his income was at least fifteen times that amount, and turned it down. He had never been to London before and the idea was appealing, but he was making a good living, and this would not be of any help in his scheme of things. The more he thought about the offer, however, he could not help but remember that James Buchanan was being considered as a presidential candidate. It would, or might be a good move, all things thought through, and maybe he should give the idea a bit more thought before letting the job fall to someone else. After a lot of soul-searching, he began seriously to reconsider.

Dan asked to meet with James Buchanan and he was invited to his home, "Wheatland," in Lancaster, Pennsylvania, for a visit, to be sized up.[1] Wheatland was, and still is, a beautiful country home, large in size, of red brick, where James Buchanan had lived happily for some time. Dan took the train to Lancaster and was met by a carriage and horses and driven to the estate. Here, Buchanan and Sickles were favorably impressed with each other. Buchanan remarked to a friend that Dan's manner, appearance, and intelligence were all that could be desired. At this time, Buchanan was sixty-two, and Dan was thirty-three. Dan was to be off on a new and possibly advantageous adventure, which could turn out to be very good indeed for his future political life.

A baby girl had been born to Dan and Teresa, the exact date not known, but in the year 1853. She was named Laura Buchanan Sickles, and was far too young to travel to England as yet, so she, her mother, Teresa, and grandmother, Mrs. Bagioli, would follow later.

Before the men left New York City, on August 6, 1853, by ship, Teresa had met and spent an evening with James Buchanan, who was charmed by Dan's wife and was looking forward to seeing her again in London as soon as it was possible. Buchanan remarked to his niece, Harriet Lane, that Teresa was a lovely young woman and her husband was a lucky man to have her. The soon-to-be United States president was unmarried, having had an unhappy affair with his fiancée, and when she suddenly died, he never married. His niece served as his official hostess from then on, in London, and in Washington.

It had been recorded in *The New York Herald* that Dan and Fanny White crossed the Atlantic, if not together, then at the same time. This meeting must have been done quietly if no suspicions were to be aroused then, especially during the time that Dan was connected with Buchanan. It was also said that Fanny was presented at court to Queen Victoria as, "Miss Bennett of New York." This was published in *The Herald,* a newspaper that attacked Sickles vigorously. Perhaps that was true, perhaps not, just published gossip.

Teresa was very unhappy and lonely without Dan, but she and their sweet baby would soon be reunited and all would be well. After Dan left, Teresa wrote to him as to her upsets during the pregnancy and continued . . .

> I hate the idea of your going away without me, and I know that I could not leave you were it in my power. You know what is best and I shall act as you wish me to, however as much as I may dislike it. God only knows how I can get along without you. God bless you, my own dear darling pet. May God bless you forever and ever is my prayer. Your truly devoted and most dearly attached wife and baby.
>
> Teresa[2]

A few months later, Teresa, her mother, and Laura arrived in London. Dan was genuinely happy to see his wife and new baby, and Teresa was delighted to see her handsome husband again.

Mrs. Bagioli took care of Laura while her daughter accompanied Dan in seeing the wonderful sights of London. The two of them were treated like royalty, and I do believe that this period was probably the highest point of their life together as husband and wife.

Teresa charmed everyone whom she met. Although only seventeen, she had lost her childish ways and was treated like a woman by the ladies she met through the American Legation.

Mr. Buchanan and Sickles were boon companions and Buchanan wrote to his friend Forney that Dan was a man of fine talents, of excellent manners, and of a brave and loyal temper. His personal relations with him had been everything he could desire. His only complaint was that Dan wrote a very bad hand and spent a great deal of money.

At this time, Mr. Buchanan was approached with the idea of considering his entry into the democratic campaign of 1856 for president of the United States. This must have repaid Dan Sickles for the loss of so much income since taking the position of secretary, to be near the man who could possibly become the next president.

Harriet Lane, Buchanan's niece, had to return to the United States on business matters dealing with some property, and as the wife of the secretary, Teresa took over the role of official hostess for James Buchanan.

This was a great honor for one so young. Rumor had it that the elderly bachelor was smitten with the beautiful wife of his secretary. Teresa's youthful simplicity and natural charm made her a favorite with the wives of Lord Palmerston and Lord Clarendon. In addition, Teresa, Harriet Lane, and Mrs. Lawrence, wife of the military attaché, were known in London as "The Three Graces." This must have been a fine time for the Sickles family, enjoying another world of success away from home and its problems.

It had become clear to Teresa as the time passed, however, that her hope of a husband true only to her would not be realized. He was kind, attentive, and brought her every indulgence, but he always reverted to being an incorrigible philanderer, with an ever-roving eye.

Mr. Buchanan hoped that Cuba could be annexed or to become part of the United States through some means, and he was not alone in pursuit of this scheme. Sickles and others were laying the groundwork for considering buying Cuba, or if that was not done by reason of its being a repugnant idea to Spanish pride, a five-million-dollar grant to the Queen Mother, Maria Christina.

Sickles went to the United States and back to London to see James Buchanan, about this, and finally to Paris and Madrid. While he was there, he was presented to the twenty-four-year-old Queen Isabella II, a lovely plump young woman notorious for her love affairs with a succession of men, after having been forced into a loveless marriage with a younger boy for political reasons to do with the throne. The queen might scarcely have noticed the young American who bowed before her. If only they had known then what would have occurred when they met a second time, when both of them were older and both scarred with the ordeals of time. They were to meet again. . . . . .

By now "Old Buck" was being pressured to run for President of the United States, and Dan Sickles was right there seconding the suggestion.

Dan, Teresa, and Laura set sail for the United States on December 6th, where he resumed his law practice, writing all the time to prominent Democrats backing James Buchanan for president in the election of 1856. They lived with the Bagiolis on East Fifteenth Street. At this time Dan and his father had law offices at 3 Nassau Street in New York City.

In the spring of 1856, James Buchanan arrived back from London after his sojourn as American ambassador, now with a plan for trying his luck as a candidate. Dan announced that he also was to run for office as congressman from the Third Congressional District of New York. Dan's income had been restored sufficiently to purchase a fine home and land on the Hudson River at Ninety-First Street in the village of Bloomingdale.[3] A country home, but still only six miles from his office, which could be easily traveled by street car or stages, which made trips all day. Dan was gone on business a lot of the time, and Teresa pined, being left alone so much of the time. She busied herself in the new home that had room for horses, cows, chickens, and all of the farm scene and gardening. Laura loved the farm and was happy to have her family around her reunited.

Still, Teresa was not the fulfilled young woman she longed to be. Her letters to friends are vague with strange emotions. She was a woman of moods.

Six

New York's Newest Congressman in Washington

Dan had been elected to Congress in the fall of 1856 by a plurality, while James Buchanan was elected president by a slim margin. He had decided to make a run for public office on a national scale and was elected along with Buchanan. This would be Dan's entry into the world he had chosen of national politics, where the real action took place. Both men were elated and eager to move to Washington. Dan was contemplating the future with his good friend in the White House. What could stand between Sickles and a promising future in government?

In Washington, before the opening of the Thirty-Fifth Congress, and while Teresa and Laura stayed in New York City, Dan took rooms at Willard's, one of the grandest of the twenty-six hotels in the city. The Willard occupied an entire block and was considered the "Most Favored Hotel in Washington." He realized that this would not be suitable once his family arrived, so he would have to find a larger home to serve as a place for his family and a place to entertain his many business and political friends and their wives.

Teresa was delighted with the thought of being the wife of a congressman. Dan was successful in dressing her in the latest fashions and jewels, and at nineteen, and as adorable as ever, she was still stunned with the realization that she could be no more to Dan than a loving wife, but whatever she did, her love alone was never enough.

Dan was even more totally into the realm of political life, which left Teresa alone more often than not, with no hint of whom he was seeing besides her. He became even more dashing, exuberant, and indulgent, happy when they were together, mainly at breakfast, and off again with a kiss and an affectionate touch. She was still a gay young woman, but Dan was not a husband. It is easy to call a marriage a mating only between the two. Where there is real love, a quiet peace descends, but without this peace, there is little to support them but trust, which she did not have. This was all the more for Teresa, never having had that period of years between schoolgirl and young matron.

Men, even strangers, took immediately to this vivacious beauty, but though pleased by the attention, this was not what she wanted. All she wished for was a devoted husband, not a man seeking new conquests, which she tried very hard to put out of her mind.

Teresa was thrust into the world of Washington society and unprepared to deal with the receptions given by the congressmen's wives. Also weekly dinner parties were held for the congressmen and their wives. Teresa's receptions were held for the wives on Tuesday mornings, and the Sickleses hosted dinner parties every Thursday evening. Teresa did finally reach an understanding of all the procedures and was able to do very well at handling the stress this involved. There was much snobbery toward some of the new congressmen's wives, by the established ladies of experienced politicians. But the real leaders of Washington society were the Southern women. This new lifestyle demanded funds to secure a place to live, so Dan rented a three-storied white brick house on Lafayette Square in

Washington.[1] This area directly faced the front of the president's house. The square was quiet, green, and convenient for visiting the White House and James Buchanan. The square was 725 feet long, 420 feet wide, and edged by an elegant fancy iron fence with gilt eagles on the gates. This fence is gone, and, since 1933, is now around the National Cemetery in Gettysburg, Pennsylvania, where lie the soldiers of the Civil War, both known and unknown.

Among other residents of Lafayette Square were financiers, noted explorers, and other government officials. The grounds of the square were originally part of the White House holdings, and the Ellipse. Later Pennsylvania Avenue was cut through the property, separating it from the White House. The square was named for the Marquis de Lafayette in 1824, and a fine statue of the gentleman on horseback is a prominent subject on view.

The house was not overly large. The ground floor contained a kitchen and an informal area for dining. On the first floor were a study or library, a parlor, a drawing room, and a large formal dining room. Upstairs were a number of bedrooms, and on the third floor were the servants' quarters. The house was built in 1820. The rent that Dan paid was $3,000 a year, which was the total salary paid a congressman. He employed a nursemaid for Laura, a coachman, a footman, a cook, and a housemaid. Dan also purchased a fine carriage, horses to pull it, and an elegant pair of riding horses for himself and Teresa. The Sickles family dog, an Italian greyhound named Dandy, also moved from New York to Washington.

The Sickleses had the house completely repainted and furnished in the latest elegant style. The pair was universally liked and their guests were welcomed with the finest in food and wines, and refined conversation. Again Teresa had quickly learned her role as hostess. She became a very important part of her husband's world, and began to fit into the political side of Washington. Her world was Dan and his world, and being a perfect wife, quiet, and taking care of any children. She was never known to express any political sentiment, as this was not to be done, out loud, anyway.

Laura was a lovely child who was happy in her new home, with a mother who gave her the desired attention, a nursemaid who helped her learn about life, and a father, whom she saw not as much as she would have liked, but a child treasures what she can understand and does not worry about the rest.

Laura's baptism was scheduled for a Sunday in mid-March 1858, and President Buchanan was to be her godfather, and Mrs. John Slidell, wife of the Senator from Louisiana, was to be Laura's godmother. Unfortunately, this important event did not take place, as Laura came down with whooping cough and there was never any mention of a later date for the baptism.[2]

Seven
A Tragedy for All Concerned

Into Dan and Teresa's life came a new character, who would alter the future for all of them. Sometimes an event with such a small beginning can change each life for better or worse, and can end in tragedy.

The advent was the person of Philip Barton Key, a captain of a company of Montgomery Guards, a military unit in Washington. Tall and handsome, uniformed in blue and gold, in a plumed hat, and he rode an iron-gray horse, Lucifer. He was an expert horseman to be sure, and made a grand appearance. He held the position of United States District Attorney for the District of Columbia, and had Dan Sickles to thank for working with President Buchanan, allowing him to be appointed again to that office. He and Dan had become friends and had met many times before, the evening dance at which Dan introduced Philip to Teresa, and Key asked Dan's wife to dance with him. Dan probably was scarcely concerned with this meeting and dancing, as he was talking with his two friends, Samuel Butterworth and Emanuel Hart.

Dan Sickles rewarded loyalty and friendship, and he liked Barton Key enough to help him keep the office he had. Key had an interesting background. His father was Francis Scott Key, who was an occasional poet and had written the words to the song that became "The Star Spangled Banner." Francis Scott Key had also held the office of

United States Attorney for the District of Columbia. Barton Key's grandfather was a Revolutionary War hero of sorts who had also married the daughter of the Governor of Virginia. Barton Key's sister was married to George Pendleton, an Ohio congressman.

Barton Key had been very happy married to Sophie Swann, but unfortunately she had died after eight years of marriage, leaving behind four small children, who were being cared for by a housekeeper in his home, while Key took off to live with his sister and her husband in their home in Washington. He pined for Sophie, was often in a state of depression, and pushed himself socially to help with this period of sorrow.

One of Barton's greatest joys was riding his hunter constantly, and he was recognized upon sight by most Washingtonians. There was many a local matron who saw a fine new son-in-law for themselves and a husband for their daughters in this handsome widower. He was a striking looking man, said to be "the Handsomest Man in Washington," with sad eyes, and a languid look, knowing how to entrance the female sex. He had once remarked to a friend that he "could get any woman to do just what he wanted after thirty-six hours with her."

It was clear that he had made an impression on Teresa, and she on him. There was an excitement felt by both of them through this meeting and physical contact. She was a small lovely woman who was also Dan Sickles's wife, and that had to be remembered. Teresa also pondered this meeting, and the next day she thought often of her feelings when his arms encircled her waist and his smiling face shone only on her, as they danced and laughed and talked as if they had known each other for years instead of minutes.

Many times Barton Key and Teresa Sickles again went dancing at some public Washington spot. This was considered perfectly all right in a city where a young matron could be squired about, especially when her husband was constantly about on business of his own, in which his wife would have no part at all. Key was considered a bachelor, and above reproach, taking care of Teresa and seeing that she arrived home safely from these nighttime pleasures.

Barton and Teresa met more often now as the affair had started slowly, but increased as opportunity presented itself. With Dan away on business or working overtime on his political bills, or spending time with other politicians to his advantage, but not to Teresa's. Little by little the affair took over most of their lives and time.

Teresa and Barton knew that they had no future together, only the stolen hours to feed their infatuation. Teresa did not want a divorce, with adultery the reason. If that was the cause, she would lose her daughter, Laura, to her father, whom the child adored. They were buying time to continue the affair, glorying in the physical contact only. All that they wanted was this fleeting contact of togetherness; they would have to settle for that.

Why would Teresa have started this affair in the first place? She truly loved Dan, had for most of her years. She felt that she could never compete with older, more worldly women whom Dan was and had been involved with. They truly loved each other, but in a different way from most husbands and wives. When Teresa met Barton Key, she was, and had been deprived of much physical contact and I believe that this stimulation and excitement became an overriding part of everyday living. This even took precedence over concern for her daughter's welfare, and this is hard to understand. She was not thinking, or caring, or desirous of anything but this strong attraction to another man.

As for Dan, he had not for one moment thought that Teresa would or could ever desire another man than himself. Say that is unrealistic, but he would have thought this way. She had adored him, possibly seduced him, and having married acted like an eager wife.

Dan did not suspect anything that was occurring in his home or the leased home so close by where the lovers met several times a week for their trysts. He had been warned by his friends that there was something going on with their involvement other than friendship, but he could not believe that his friend and his wife were behaving as he was told.

Teresa's friends knew of the total involvement and warned her that trouble was about to descend on her family, but that did no good.

Finally Dan told Teresa that he did not want Key invited to the house.

The Sickles's servants, Bridget Duffy, the housemaid, and John Thompson, the coachman, became aware of the comings and goings of Mr. Key at the Sickles home, and in May, Mr. Sickles was away on his frequent business trips. They both saw the mistress and Mr. Key in the small library and heard the door locked on either side of the room at about 1:00 A.M. The two servants retired to their respective rooms, believing that they each knew what was transpiring in the library.

In July, the Sickleses closed their Washington home for the summer recess in Washington and returned to New York and Bloomingdale. Dan was glad to see his old friends, Emanuel Hart, Samuel Butterworth, Charles K. Graham, Thomas Francis Meagher, James Brady, and August Belmont. They were lawyers and politicians whom he trusted and respected, and they were fiercely loyal to Dan, and he to them. They all recognized that he had a fine future ahead of him. During the summer, Barton Key had stopped at the Bloomingdale home for a short nervous visit on his way to Saratoga, New York. The summer was quiet for Dan, Teresa, and Laura. A time to think hard, but with an undercurrent of possible trouble in the return to Washington in the early fall.

The Sickleses left New York and reopened the Washington home. And their servants and countless pieces of baggage made the trip also.

The summer had given Teresa a breathing spell, long enough to relax, but there was contemplation for Teresa of what might happen later. Dan had almost forgotten about the trouble he had gone through questioning Key and his wife, so he put it out of his mind. Barton Key had assured Dan that he had only the friendliest sort of affection for Teresa, as he thought of her as almost a child. Dan believed his words and so other thoughts took precedence over any complication such as that.

Barton Key returned to Washington to stay again with the Pendletons and see his four children, who still lived at his home with the housekeeper. He belonged to a club, also on Lafayette Park, called the Club House, where Washington men in the government met with friends for drinks and to discuss local gossip.

That winter the old Stockton mansion was lighted with brilliant soirees, dinners, and parties. Dan was living in great style, and Teresa was dressed beautifully and was living up to her role as mistress of the house in all respects.

There is a lovely reference to Teresa that was published as written here.

> She was so young and fair, at most not more than twenty-two years of age, and so naive, that none of the party of

which I was, one was willing to harbor a belief in the rumors which were then in circulation, on that, Mrs. Sickles last "at home." Her parlors were thronged, one half a hundred or more guests being men. The girl hostess was even more lovely than usual. Of an Italian type of feature and coloring, she was the daughter of a famous musician, Bagioli, of New York. Mrs. Sickles was dressed in a painted muslin gown, filmy and graceful, on which the outlines of crocus might be traced. A broad sash of brocaded ribbon girdled her slender waist and in her dark hair was yellow crocus blooms. I never saw her again, but the picture of which she formed the center so fair and innocent, it fixed itself permanently upon my mind.[1]

Barton Key and Teresa no longer made such secretive plans as before. Neither of them seemed to care not to show the private side of their relationship to the world. He was very careful when Dan was at home, but when he was absent, caution was thrown to the wind and he was at the Sickles home constantly. Barton found a house to rent for the meetings with Teresa, which he deemed the thing to do for the privacy he wanted. This was a small sparsely furnished house in a racially mixed neighborhood just three blocks away from the Sickles home. A load of cut firewood was delivered to warm the house and the neighbors saw smoke rising from the chimney every few days. Many a window curtain was parted to gaze at the goings on at the house, seeing that at least one of the occupants was known. Mr. Key arrived on his gray mount, Lucifer.

Teresa was not known, but they could see that the same woman arrived each time with her head bowed and her cloak pulled up to her face. Barton would have come by the Sickles house and waved a white handkerchief at Teresa's bedroom window. Barton would use binoculars to see if Teresa knew he was there. At this signal, Teresa would leave the house and walk the ten-minute walk to the house at number 383 Fifteenth Street. After an interval of an hour or more, the woman would leave and shortly after that, the man would leave after locking the door.

John Cooney took the position of coachman from John Thompson, and he also became aware of a thinly veiled conspiracy of the by-now lovers. By mid-winter the "affair" was known by the majority of people in Washington, except for Dan Sickles. Other friends beseeched both Barton and Teresa to desist and be warned that very real physical danger could result unless a stop was made to this affair.

Around this time, Dan had met Edwin Stanton, another lawyer, who found Dan to be warm and friendly. Stanton's wife, Ellen, was only twenty-nine years old to her husband's forty-six, so he and Dan had more than one reason to become simpatico. Thus began a friendship that could last through many years of personal and political grief. Edwin Stanton would play an important part in shaping the fortunes of Daniel Sickles.

On Thursday evening February 24, 1859, the Sickles were to give the last of the dinner parties, although they did not know it at the time. Barton Key was not invited because of friction between Dan and Teresa concerning his presence in their home. At the party was Octavia Ridgeley, Teresa's one dear friend and eighteen years old. The party ended about ten P.M. and most of the guests left to go to Willard's where a dance was being given as usual each evening.

Teresa left with Octavia, and Dan was to follow when all of the remaining guests had left the house. Before Dan left, he decided to look over the mail that had arrived that day, which he had not seen. One was an envelope of a cheap yellow, and not the usual type he would have received. It took him only a few seconds to open and read it, and stagger emotionally at the words.

Washington, February 24, 1859
Hon. Daniel Sickles,
Dear Sir,

With great regret I enclose to your address the few lines, but an indispensable duty compels me so to do seeing that you are greatly imposed upon.

There is a fellow I may say, for he is not a gentleman, by the name of Philip Barton Key and I believe, the district attorney, who rents a house of a Negro man by the name of Jno. A. Gray situated on 15th Street between K and L Streets, for no other purpose than to meet your wife, Mrs. Sickles. He hangs a string out of the window as a signal to her that he is in and leaves the door unfastened and she walks in and sir I do assure you with these few hints, I leave the rest for you to imagine.

Most respectfully,

Your Friend R.P.G.[2]

Dan had not for one moment thought that Teresa would ever desire another man than he himself. Say that he was unrealistic, but he would have thought this. She had adored him, and said so, and acted like an eager wife. He had had it all, her dear love for long years since she was a child growing up, and the love and adoration of countless women since he was a grown man. What had gone so wrong? I am sure at this juncture he was truly troubled by this newly understood knowledge. He thought of no wife for himself or mother to his child, than Teresa. Why, had she been involved for so long without his noticing it?

It is not known if he went to Willard's or stayed home that evening. He left the house on Friday morning, greatly agitated, and walked to see for himself the house mentioned in the letter, and asked questions of some of the neighbors. From there he walked to the offices of the two Washington papers, *The Daily States,* and *The Evening Star,* to have inserted for the next day's edition a personal message as follows.

> R.P.G., who recently addressed a letter to a gentleman in this city, will confer a great favor upon the gentleman to whom the letter was addressed by granting him an early, immediate, and confidential interview.[3]

Dan showed the letter he had received to his friend and House clerk, George Wooldridge, and began to read the words but could not continue without too much emotion to be noticed in the congressional halls. They then went into an anteroom where Sickles became completely overcome. He voiced the hope that the woman would be found not to have been Teresa. He implored his friends to go to the house, he would show him the way, and ask more questions of the neighbors. This was done in secret. The descriptions of the woman fit Teresa perfectly as to dress. The servants were questioned and they told what they knew of the affair. They mentioned the waving of the white handkerchief many times. Dan's look was mentioned by a passing friend as wild, desolate, and defiant.

That evening at home, Dan was so visibly upset that he requested a tray be sent to his room. Teresa could see that something was very wrong with him. She could not ask what the problem was as she was entertaining her friend, Octavia Ridgeley, for the weekend. Dan asked Teresa to come to his room, and then Miss Ridgeley and the servants heard loud talk and sobbing from both husband and wife. His groans were awful, like the wailing of a Greek chorus. Dan was never one to hold his emotions inside himself, and the doubts and fears surfaced all at once.

Teresa's mostly happy life had come to an abrupt end at age twenty-two! By nine o'clock, Dan had asked Teresa and Bridget, the maid, and Octavia to come to the room and witness a paper that Teresa had just written. Teresa sat solemnly with her head bowed, a handkerchief against her eyes. Dan also was weeping with emotion, almost uncontrollably. The handwriting was in her girlish hand that reads as follows. . . .

> I have been in the house in Fifteenth Street with Mr. Key. How many times I don't know. I believe the house belongs to a colored man. The house is unoccupied. Commenced going there the later part of January. Have been in alone and with Mr. Key. Usually stayed an hour or more. There was a bed in the second story. I did what is usual for a wicked woman to do.
>
> The intimacy commenced this winter, when I came from New York, half a dozen times or more, at different hours of the day. On Monday of this week, and Wednesday also, I would arrange meetings when we met in the street and at parties. Never would I speak to him when Mr. Sickles was at home, because I knew he did not like me to speak to him; I did not see Mr. Key for some days after I got here. He then told me that he had hired the house as a place where he and I could meet. I agreed to it. Had nothing to eat or drink there. The room is warmed by a wood fire.
>
> Mr. Key usually goes first. Have walked there together say four times, I do not think more, was there on Wednesday last, between two and three. I went there alone. Laura was at Mrs. Hoover's. Mr. Key took her there at my request. From there I went to Fifteenth Street to meet Mr. Key; from there to the milk woman's. Immediately after Mr. Key left Laura at Mrs. Hoover's, I met him in Fifteenth Street. Went in by the back gate. Went to the same bedroom, and there an improper interview was had. I undressed myself. Mr.

Key undressed also. This occurred on Wednesday, 23rd of February, 1859.

Mr. Key had kissed me in this house a number of times. I do not deny that we have had connection in this house, last Spring, a year ago in the parlor, and on the sofa. Mr. Sickles was sometimes out of town, and sometimes in the Capitol. I think the intimacy commenced in April or May, 1858. I did not think it safe to meet him in this house because there are servants who might suspect something. As a general rule have worn a black silk dress, also a plaid dress, and a black and white woolen dress. A black velvet cloak trimmed with lace, and a black velvet shawl trimmed with fringe. On Wednesday I either had on my brown dress or black and white woolen dress, beaver hat and velvet shawl.

I arranged with Mr. Key to go in the back way after leaving Laura at Mrs. Hoover's. He met me at Mr. Douglas's as we would be less likely to be seen. The house is on Fifteenth Street between K and L Streets, on the left hand side of the street, I think. I went in the front door, it was open, occupied the same room, undressed myself, and he also; went to bed together. Mr. Key has ridden in Mr. Sickles's carriage, and has called at his house without Mr. Sickles's knowledge, and after my being told not to invite him to do so, and against Mr. Sickles's repeated request."[4]

Teresa Bagioli

This is a true statement, written by myself, without any inducement held out by Mr. Sickles of forgiveness or reward, and without any menace from him. This I have written with my bedroom door open, and my maid and child in the adjoining room, at half past eight o'clock in the evening. Miss Ridgeley is in the house, within call.

Teresa Bagioli
Lafayette Square, Washington, D.C., Feb. 26, 1859

Mr. and Mrs. Pendleton dined here two weeks ago last Thursday, with a large party. Mr. Key was here also, her brother, and at my suggestion he was invited, because he lived in the same house, and Mr. Sickles wished to invite all those from whom he had received invitations: and Mr. Sickles said, "Do as you choose."

Teresa Bagioli

Written and signed in the presence of O.M. Ridgeley and Bridget Duffy
Feb. 26th, 1859

Octavia M. Ridgeley
Bridget Duffy[5]

No one responded to Dan's personal message in either newspaper. The mystery of whom the initials R.P.G. stood for would never be solved. Some thought it to be the handwriting of a woman.

Dan had taken Teresa's wedding ring from her and broken it in two. There was little sleep in the Sickles home that night. Octavia was afraid for Teresa, who spent the night in her friend's room, on the floor, with her head resting on a small chair. Octavia did not understand completely what was happening as Teresa was not one to confide in even her best friend, so the meaning of all of the anguish was not known at once.

Dan arose and all could hear unearthly groans coming from him. He was pacing and holding his head, sobbing uncontrollably.

Barton had no idea of the events that had transpired the night before, and he spruced up with a shave and a hair trim at Willard's, before heading over to Lafayette

Square. The Sunday was warm for February, even in Washington. He was seen approaching Pennsylvania Avenue.

A good friend of Dan's and a Tammany cohort, Samuel Butterworth, who lived in New York City, but was visiting Washington, received a short note,

> Dear B.
> Come to me right away.
> Dan[6]

Samuel Butterworth could not imagine what this meant, but he hurried to the Sickles home. Dan was prostrate with grief on his bed and blurted out the whole sordid story. Dan was seeking his advice, which was to send Teresa to her mother and then plan a separation to be arranged. This would take time to get done, but it was the right approach. Samuel went downstairs to give Dan some time alone after giving his advice, and he was shown by Woolridge the note that Teresa had written, telling of the confession. Butterworth left with a message to Dan that he would return soon.

The Sickles dog, Dandy, had gotten loose somehow, and ran to Key when he approached and started to play with the waving handkerchief that Baron was waving as a distraction. Finally Dandy tired of the game and ran off.

Dan just happened to pass the window, saw Key waving the handkerchief, and he almost went crazy, saying, "That villain has just passed my house and is making signals, My God! This is horrible!" By that time Butterworth had returned and, together with Dan, looked on. Dan was calmed but only to a point, as he said that all the city knew of his affair. Butterworth said that it might be kept quiet and it should not be made any more public for the sake of Dan's career.

Butterworth told him, "There is but one honorable course left to you, you need no advice." This either meant a duel or something more permanent. Dan went to his room and picked out two derringers and a single revolver that he owned, also taking a hat and black frock coat from the hall rack. Dan was headed for the Clubhouse.

Lafayette Square was filled with Sunday strollers, couples, and men alone or in groups visiting the park. At least twelve people tell the following event in different versions, but the essential details are the same. Dan got Butterworth to walk ahead and detain Key with a short conversation to delay his progress until Dan had arrived, which he did very soon. Dan faced the man and shouted, "Key, you scoundrel, you have dishonored my house. You must die." Dan fired after he noticed that Key had put his hand in his jacket front as if to obtain a gun possibly. Barton was grazed but not hurt badly, and grabbed Dan from behind.

Dan broke away, pulled out another gun from his coat pocket, and pointed it at Key, who yelled out, "Don't murder me!" Barton turned to run away and tossed something at Dan, which turned out to be the field glasses that he used to watch for Teresa at her window to see if she had understood the signal. This last bullet found its mark in Key's groin, just missed a main artery, passed into the thigh, and exited in a section between the thigh and buttock. "I am shot," Barton shouted, "Don't shoot me."

Dan shouted, "You villain, you have dishonored my house, and you must die." Dan came at him again, trying to fire, but the gun misfired. Dan cocked it again, put the gun barrel to Key's chest and fired. This time Key was mortally wounded. Dan put the gun to Key's head and fired, but the gun misfired a second time. The damage had been done before this last shot when the bullet had hit between the ribs, through the spleen, and into the hipbone.

Dan asked, "Is the scoundrel dead? He has violated my bed. He has defiled my bed, He has dishonored my bed!"

Meanwhile, Butterworth had watched this appalling spectacle and had not tried to stop the action, but now that it was over, he took hold of Dan and the two of them walked quietly up the street. Although Butterworth was an eyewitness, he was never called for any evidence at the trial that was to follow.

Key was barely alive, was carried to The Clubhouse, and placed on the floor with his shoulders propped up on an overturned chair. Key made no answer as to his last words to his four children, and very soon after that he died.

What could possibly have made Dan ask his wife to write her own "death sentence"? A man whose house was dishonored by a wayward wife while he, in Victorian times, had dallied with many women. This was considered the double standard, which we still have today. Teresa's self-respect had vanished, for she had been caught and more public scandal would be forthcoming as word of the tragedy. Her own confession would be published in newspapers across the country and in Europe. Daniel Sickles, being a lawyer and gathering evidence, probably wanted this document not to expedite a divorce, but as punishment for the year or more of hidden involvement between Barton and Teresa. If violence was to occur with Key, because of this, then Dan would have evidence of her infidelity, and in her own handwriting to prove the reason. Teresa was shamed before all.

Later during the court trial, this evidence that she had written was not allowed to be used against her. She was not called at all, and was in no condition to be called as a witness. "Those who have known her," said *The New York Times,* "will grieve sorely at the necessity of giving her up as lost."[7] *Harper's Weekly* published poetry about her as follows. . .

Bridle your virtue, tether your tongue
Pity the fair vine, blighted so young.
Why not the tomb? sad shattered life.
Think of her doom, widow, yet wife.[8]

Barton Key was buried in the Presbyterian Cemetery in Baltimore, next to his wife. His brother and other family members were overheard making threats against Daniel Sickles, and there was talk of revenge, but talk only.

It must be added here that at no time was it considered that Dan would be held accountable for his actions of killing his wife's lover. No one expected anything other than a justifying conclusion as to his actions. He was the cuckold husband of an unfaithful wife and had sympathy from the entire country.

Dan was delivered to the Washington jail, small, smelly, and a place not fit for the friend of President Buchanan, so pressure was finally brought to have him moved, which was done, and he was given the warden's own rooms.

Dan had refused bail for himself, wanting the trial to start as soon as possible. His dog, Dandy, was even allowed to stay in his quarters as a companion. His friends arrived en masse; even his father came from New York quickly, annoyed yet afraid for the future of his son, nothing new there! Letters of condolence arrived daily in volume, one from the president, many from strangers who championed his cause. The newspapers made long daily comments on any of the latest findings, and after a while, they were speculating only and disliked losing a fine scandalous story to print and also losing readers who enjoy such delight in other people's misery, fortunate that it is not their problem.

Dan requested that his minister visit him Rev. E.H. Haley, who lived close by the jail and did so daily. He became a go-between with Teresa, bringing her, bringing Dan news of his wife, who was obsessed by guilt and grieving for the shame for her daughter, Laura, an innocent child in all of this sordid tale. Teresa was almost suicidal, would not eat, slept not well at all. She had begged the Rev. Haley to allow Dan to return her wedding ring to her, which he had taken the night she wrote the letters and had broken in two in front of her, and she wanted it back, broken or not.

Dan agreed to the return of the ring, but under the condition that he would never see her again. The Bagiolis arrived to see their daughter, who was now in a dangerous state of collapse. Mrs. Bagioli took Teresa and Laura back with her to New York City in March, when it was agreed that Teresa could make the trip and it might help to get away from Washington. However, all the insecurities went along with all of them; only now they were farther away, which helped and hurt. Before they left, Laura was allowed to see her "Papa." Dan tried to explain why he was in this "new office," but Laura could sense something was wrong. She was going on six years old and it was not as easy to fool her now. Both she and her father wept when they said good-bye.

Dan's friends saw to it that decent meals, even wine, were sent from nearby taverns and restaurants for his pleasure. Octavia Ridgley, upon word from Teresa, sent him a box full of clothes, cigars, books, pens, and paper. Dan's lawyers arrived from New York City, with James T. Brady, as head of the defense, with Edwin M. Stanton, and John Graham, assisting Brady.

Dan had many friends, but also many enemies. One of the worst against him was *The New York Evening Post,* an example as follows . . .

> The wretched man, Daniel E. Sickles, has in his career reached the stage of assassination, and dipped his hands in human blood. . . . He is a person of notorious profligacy of life . . . a certain disgrace has for years past attended the reputation of being one of his companions. . . . Sickles was excluded from decent society in this city long ago; and it would be almost a miracle if in the school to which he took his young wife, she should have preserved her innocence. . . . It is certain that the man who makes no scruples to invade and destroy the domestic peace of others, he who, in his own practice, regards adultery as a joke and the matrimonial bond no barrier against the utmost caprice of licentiousness, has little right to complain when the mischief which he carries without scruple into other families enters his own.[9]

Thus "The Washington Tragedy" became common knowledge. There were drawings of all elements of the story, as photography was not used in many papers at that time. The big question was "Does a man have the right to shoot and kill the seducer of his wife?"

One month from the shooting, Teresa writes to Dan . . . plaintive loving letters filled with remorse and true feeling.

> Good morning, dear, dear, Dan—Mr. Fields has just left. He brought me a kind, good letter from you. Thank you many times for all your kind expressions and God bless you for the mercy and prayers you offer up for me. Do not ask if I never think over the events of the past month. Yesterday, at each hour by the clock, I thought, "one month ago this day, at this hour, such and such things were going on in our once happy home." That fearful Saturday night! No one has any idea what I suffered. If I could have foreseen the scenes of the following day, I would have braved all dangers, all things to have prevented them. Oh, that Manny Hart could have been with us!

I have been out of the house but three times since I came home; and you know how much exercise I have been in the habit of taking. . . . Last night I walked with Manny Hart; but my body trembled, my legs seemed to give way under me, and my heart beat violently.

The verses you sent me are very beautiful. I will keep them always, and I thank you for them sincerely. . . . Perhaps I spoke hastily of George Woolridge, I promise not to mention his name, Wiley or Butterworth again in any of my letters unless necessary. One thing I will assure you of, and that is that I did not tell Mr. Butterworth to mind his own business or anything to that effect. . . . Mr. Butterworth, I think, only needed encouragement from me to flirt. I may be mistaken, but I doubt it. But let all suppositions be forgotten and unthought of; the reality is bad enough without suspecting or supposing things. . . .

No, Dear Dan, I cannot say that you ever denied me what was necessary, and you gave me many things that I did not deserve, everyone knows this. I shall commence a pair of slippers for you in a few days, my dear Dan. I will not stop working on them until they are finished. Will you wear them for me? Or would you dislike to wear anything that I have made?

Can I say or do anything for you that you have not spoken of—if so, write me. Do not be angry at anything I have written you. I swear that I have not written a word to cause you pain . . . write me when you can, and think and feel as leniently as possible of me and my unhappy position. God bless you for the two kisses you send me—and with God's help and my own determination to be good, true, and faithful to you and myself hereafter, those kisses shall never leave my lips while I am called WIFE and you HUSBAND. I swear it by Laura. . . . God bless you, pray for me, and believe in the sincerity and gratitude of Teresa.[10]

Another letter written during the trial. . . .

I cannot tell you, dear, dear Dan, how MUCH pleasure your letter written yesterday gave me. I am so glad the flowers were acceptable. You are so wrong in supposing that I was pained at your silence, and equally pained at receiving the letter you sent me. You know, Dan, I never affect to love or dislike a person, and I am, in a certain way, as frank as any breathless creature. You say that if I can hate those whom you love and who love you then it is vain for you to appeal to me again on such a subject. Dear Dan, it would be impossible for me to love those who hate me and have injured me, have called me every vile name, as I believe it would be to have you love me again or ever to wipe out the past. I enclose a letter written last night. I send it to you now to show you how I felt about all you said. IT TELLS THE FEARFUL STORY OF MY HEART.

You say that any object you love remains dear to you. Do I stand upon a footing with the other women I know you have loved? I have long felt like asking you what your love affairs have been—love of the heart, or love of their superior qualities such as you have often informed me that I did not possess, or attraction of face and form, or an infatuation? If during the first years we were married my good conduct did not keep you true to me, can I suppose for a moment the last year has? ASK YOUR OWN HEART WHO SINNED FIRST, THEN TELL ME, IF YOU WILL.[11]

Certainly this plaintive plea does not sound like a non-loving wife. . . .

And the mention of many letters and beautiful verses do not show an uncaring husband in Dan. A very strange sort of relationship to exist after such violence in human behavior. Teresa is not the childlike waif anymore, but a mature woman with a "way with words," knowing exactly how to state facts and questions.

Eight

Hunkered Down in Congress; the Lowest Point

Daniel Sickles went on trial on April 4th, 1859. He had eight important lawyers, four of whom were friends. The prosecution had one man, Robert Ould, formerly assistant to Key, now replacing the murdered man as prosecutor of the office of District Attorney, by the president's appointment. At the last moment, another attorney was added to Mr. Ould's staff, being paid "out of pocket" by the friends of Barton Key.

The prosecutor, although a rather quiet man, started out at full steam, but was outclassed by Edwin Stanton, the head trial lawyer for Sickles, and the other attorneys defending Dan. Dan was seen as a man made temporarily insane by rage at the thought of a good friend seducing his very young wife, and right under his nose, at that! Dan appeared tense and unnerved by the endless details of the shame put on him over and over again. He lost his composure several times hearing the story retold. Once the trial was stopped long enough for Dan to compose himself so that testimony could resume.

The prosecution had several examples of infidelity on Dan's part, such as a tryst at Barnum's Hotel in Baltimore by Dan and a lady with him, but this was never introduced.[1] If you have heard the good conduct assigned to

Dan before the jury, you would have believed that he was a one-woman man himself!

Teresa was dragged down into the muddy bottom, being called a prostitute by one defense attorney.

Dan's friends visited him daily, and saw that foods and wines that he liked were delivered to the jail, along with a heavy volume of letters addressed to him by friends and strangers alike. There was much to keep him busy and his mind occupied. He was even allowed to have his dog, Dandy, serve the sentence with him until the end. Teresa sent flowers, which he had always liked, to the room. It should be reemphasized that Dan was not in a jail cell, but rather in the quarters of the superintendent, as the jail itself was a miserable place, dirty, cold, and loathsome. His jailor became a good friend during the stay and was glad for him, but unhappy to lose his company when he left.

It is interesting to learn that the only two women in the courtroom were those called to testify, including Bridget Duffy, the housemaid. None were on the jury, of course, but not a woman spectator was in the courtroom. I guess that women were not meant to learn about justice to them or for them at this period in American life.

By April 26th, Dan was acquitted of the murder due to temporary insanity, the first use of such a plea of jurisprudence in the United States. When word of the acquittal by the jury was announced, jubilation took over and joyous crowds closed in on Dan. His father sobbed openly. Edwin Stanton was actually dancing a little jig in the courtroom, and all were congratulating Dan, who finally reached the jury box to thank the jurors for his safe deliverance. Meanwhile, the crowds outside heard the shouting from inside the courthouse, with people hurrying about to deliver the good news further. There was much emotional excitement, and Dan was filled with wonder as more and more strangers clasped his hands and shouted their joy at his acquittal and release. This murder trial was the most important trial to take place in Washington before the Civil War.

That night at the National Hotel, a party was held by the lawyers, and the Marine Band played on the street, and they along with many thousands of men and women marched down Pennsylvania Avenue to Willard's Hotel to play for one of the lawyers who was staying there, John Graham. Dan had left for Lafayette Square, but to stay with a friend at his home, a neighbor, John McBlair. Dan had won the sympathy of the entire nation.

He had proved that when one man violates the honor and home of one of his neighbors, he does so at the peril of his life, and if violence occurs, by the outraged husband's hands, the man is liable for his own doom.

Teresa was shamed so publicly in order to release Dan from the murder charge, that she was snubbed and taunted, and kept from the public eye. Only their good friend, Emanuel Hart, gave her sympathy, caring, and support when she needed him. He had taken over the running of the Washington House until Teresa left with her mother and Laura for New York and even went there to help her cope with the changes.

Dan notified the Stockton Mansion owner that he would not be returning to the house again, and shut the door, no longer a tenant in Washington. He had been re-elected, so he was not worried about standing still for scrutiny from the electorate. He returned to Bloomingdale, to rest and regain his serenity in quiet along the Hudson River.

During the summer, there was a rumor circulating that Dan was seeing Teresa again, and taking her on boat rides on the river. No one could believe this story who knew how he felt about refusing to see his wife again. Dan, given some time to reconsider how he felt about the future, and seeing some blame for the separation of himself and Teresa, still thought of her as his wife. He wept openly and even found some solace in religion.

His former lawyers and friends urged him to think of his position. He was wronged, reacted violently, was exonerated, and now was forgiving her to the doom of his political career. If he forgave her now, why did he insist on killing Key? To portray Teresa as a "bad woman" and then take her back as before! Sheer lunacy for certain and an end to a career.

Now hearing about the possible reconciliation between Dan and Teresa, the newspapers and public were unbelieving and even hostile. Now the hero was the dead Philip Barton Key! Why was he killed? What were the reasons for Dan to forgive his wife whom the trial lawyers had vilified unmercifully? Even some of Dan's friends were disgusted by the sudden change and forgiveness that they believed could never take place. Dan had been duped—the jury had been duped, the public had been duped. One paper, *The Sunday Mercury,* printed a poem about an unnamed couple, but all knew who the parties were.

Hail! Matchless pair. United once again
In new born bliss forget your bygone pain
Hail! Turtle doves, returning to the nest
Defiled, yet dear—determined to be blest!
What though the world may say, With hands all red
Yon bridegroom steals to a dishonored bed.
And friends, estranged, explain on every side:
Behold! Adultery couched with Homicide!
What thought, in dreams a bleeding spectra flings
Your curtains backward, like a demon's wings,
And howls, exulting, as entranced you lie

Beneath the glare of its sardonic eye;
Live on—live on! Each other's proper Hell
None but yourselves could damn yourselves so well![2]

Dan was livid about anyone's right to address his family's life, and his daughter's mother. He wrote a letter to the editor of *The Herald,* which was published throughout the nation. Here are the words that he had so beautifully documented as his beliefs for the world to see.

> Through the course of sad events, which during the last few months have brought so much affliction upon my family, I have been silent. No amount of misrepresentation affecting myself only could induce me to open my lips; nor could I deem it worthwhile under any circumstances to notice what has been or can be said in journals never regarded as the source or the exponents of public opinion, for in these it is too often obvious that only unworthy motives prompt the most vindictive assaults upon the private life of citizens holding public stations. But the editorial comments in *The Herald* of yesterday, although censorious, of which I do not complain, whilst I read them with regret, differ so widely in tone and temper from the mass of nonsense and calumny which have lately been written regarding a recent event in my domestic relations, that I cannot allow a mistake into which you have been led by inaccurate information, to pass without such a correction as will relieve others from any share of the reproaches which it is the pleasure of the multitude at this moment to heap upon me and mine.
>
> Referring to the forgiveness which my sense of duty and my feelings impelled me to extend to an erring and repentant wife, you observe, in the course of your temperate and dignified article, that, "It is said, however, that the last phase of the affair was brought about through the advice of his lawyers." This is entirely erroneous. I did not exchange a word with one of my counsel upon the subject, nor with

anyone else. My reconciliation with my wife was my own act, done without consultation with any relative, connection, friend, or advisor. Whatever blame, if any belongs to the step, should fall alone upon me. I am prepared to defend what I have done before any tribunal I recognize as having the slightest claim to jurisdiction over the subject—my own conscience and the bar of Heaven. I am not aware of any statute, or code of morals, which makes it infamous to forgive a woman; not is it unusual to make our domestic life a subject of consultation with friends, no matter how near and dear to us. And I cannot allow even all the world combined to dictate to me the repudiation of my wife, when I think it right to forgive her, and restore her to my confidence and protection.

If I ever failed to comprehend the utterly desolate position of an offending though penitent woman—the hopeless future, with its dark possibilities of danger, to which she is doomed when proscribed as an outcast—I can now see plainly enough, in the almost universal howl of denunciation with which she is followed to my threshold, the misery and perils from which I have rescued the mother of my child. And although it is very sad for me to incur the blame of friends and the reproaches of many wise and good people, I shall strive to prove to all who may feel an interest in me, that if I am the first man who has ventured to say to the world an erring wife and mother may be forgiven and redeemed, that, in spite of the example shall entitle it to the imitation of the generous, and the condemnation of the just.

There are many who think that an act of duty, proceeding solely from affections which can only be comprehended in the heart of a husband and father, is to be fatal to my profession, political, and social standing. If this be so, then so be it. Political station, professional success, social recognition, are not the only prizes of ambition, and I have seen enough of the lives of others to teach me that, if one be patient and resolute. It is the man himself who indicates the place he will occupy, and as long as I do nothing worse than reunite my family under the roof where they will find shelter from contumely and persecution. I do not fear the noisy but fleeting voice of popular clamor. The multitude accept their first impressions from a few; but in the end men think for themselves, and if I know the heart—and sometimes I think that in a career of mingled sunshine and storm I have sounded nearly all its depths—then I may assure those who look with reluctant forebodings upon my future to be of good cheer, for I will not cease to vindicate just claim to the respect of my fellows; while to those motley groups, here and there, who look upon my misfortunes only as weapons to be employed for my destruction, to those I say, once and for all, if a man make a good use of his enemies, they will be as serviceable to him as his friends. In conclusion, let me ask only one favor of those who, from whatever motive, may deem it necessary or agreeable to comment in public or private upon my sad history; and that is, to aim their arrows at my breast, and for the sake of my innocent child, to spare her yet youthful mother, while she seeks in sorrow and contrition the mercy and pardon of HIM to whom, sooner or later, we must all appeal."[3]

It would have been wonderful if this reunion had been a real one, a penitent wife forgiven, a loving husband, realizing his lack of attention to his wife, a child, again living with her mother and father, in love with each other and shielding her from any further harm, this love producing other children to fill their home and hearts. A happy ending of the story of the beautiful princess and her older Prince Charming, who would live happily ever after. This is what Teresa must have visualized, but Dan could not and never would.

This could have been a turning point in all three lives, but it was never to happen. Events would shape Dan's decision to return to a more normal family life through all his good intentions, which he gave to the world via the newsprint. Take her back, he did. Protect her, he could not. Give their child a happy home, not to be. Teresa could not be happy living this way without Dan's love, and so Laura, as she grew up, was like a one-parent orphan. Her father went his separate way, leaving his "two children" alone together. It was his decision and one for which he might possibly rue the day he made it.

This quietness and humility could last just so long for Dan. Time was healing for him, and the nation was beginning to come apart! The southern states were talking secession and there was much confusion as to which way states and politicians would turn. Dan no longer felt that silence was beneficial for him. President Buchanan wanted mediation at all costs and neither side would tolerate that decision. James Buchanan did not possess the strength that this situation required, with the crisis coming soon. But Dan Sickles thrived on this kind of challenge, whether it be political, financial, or sexual.

Dan had always admired George Washington, so he had submitted a resolution making George Washington's birthday a national holiday throughout the land. The resolution was passed through the efforts of Dan Sickles, to honor "The Father of Our Country."

By April, 1861, Dan was back in the law office of his father on Nassau Street in New York City. This was a low point for him, because he had progressed so far, only a few years ago, and at almost forty-two years of age, he now seemed to be back where he started. Although he had not been able to get past actually forgiving Teresa, he still found other women very appealing. Teresa felt much guilt about what had happened to her husband's career, since he had publicly decided on reunion. She was very depressed, unable to sleep well, and resorted to opiates to seek oblivion.

President James Buchanan lost the Democratic Party nomination for president in the fall election of 1860, and with a sense of relief, left the madness of Washington for his beloved Wheatland, in Lancaster, Pennsylvania, on March 4th, 1861. He had enough of politics, especially with war threatening on the steps of the White House. He longed for the peace and tranquility of his old familiar home.

Now Abraham Lincoln, a Republican, would have to deal with the largest political crisis since the American war of revolution. Dan's friends, and his head trial lawyer, Edwin Stanton, was now Attorney General under Buchanan, soon to be Lincoln's Secretary of War.

War did finally erupt with the firing on Fort Sumter. Teresa had heard a rumor that her husband was determined to enlist, even as a private. However, Dan had spent many years in the New York State National Guard and would take an officer's position. She begged him to come home, adding news about the condition of the estate in Bloomingdale, that Dandy was a "pitiful" sight to behold, that a pack of rats were gnawing at the wood of the home somewhere. Her letters were newsy, and many hugs and kisses were sent from Laura, now almost seven years old. She ended her letter, "Dear, dear Dan, write soon and often. Let me know when we may expect you home. God bless and protect you, Dear Dear Dan, and believe me your sincerely attached wife, Teresa."[4]

Dan sometimes used questionable methods to gain his goals, but when he used sincere and honest tactics, the outcome was not what he expected. Reportedly all through the years, he was the ultimate opportunist, a man who took advantage of opportunities or circumstances with little regard for principles or consequences. In my opinion, some of this is true, but not all of it, As war descended on the United States, he had been conciliatory to the South before, but now could see that the future lay with the North, and the cause of the Union, not disunion.

The first session of the Thirty-Sixth Congress began on December 5, 1859. After the trial, Dan was no longer a power to be reckoned with in the Democratic Party, as he was considered more of an embarrassment then a help to his congressional allies. He was shunned by some of his former Democratic Tammany cohorts, so he sat off "in a corner," listening to all the proceedings and voting quietly. He was not even considering running for a third election. Why, even his good friend President Buchanan, stayed away from him. . . . He had his own problems. . . . Dan arrived each day dressed finely, but stayed to himself. It depressed him to appear so almost humble, as it was not in his nature, but he was feeling what had to be his less than usual flamboyant self after all of the crisis in his life had just occurred and a great toll on him.

Dan no longer lived on Lafayette Square, but in an apartment on Thirteenth Street, a few blocks away from his former home.

Teresa and Laura were of course living in the Bloomingdale home in New York. Her parents were there most of the time, to see that their daughter had at least some family near and the support that she needed so badly. Her parents had always stood behind her, but her father, especially, was deeply shaken by the shooting and the trial. Both Mr. Bagioli and Dan's father, George Garrett Sickles, had sat together every day of the trial to form a united family behind Dan. Each of their children was an only child, so they could give the undivided attention together. As I said before, there were no women at the trial except for two witnesses, so it must have been hard on the two mothers to be far away and quite out of touch with what was going on in the courthouse each day that it lasted.

Nine
Duty, Honor, and Country

Dan and Captain William Wiley, a Tammany member and crony, who had stood behind him at the trial, and embraced Dan at the very moment of acquittal, met at Delmonico's for a drink where they met other acquaintances and in due course, the talk turned to the war. Captain Wiley suggested to Dan that they should raise a company or a regiment of volunteers to aid in the defense of the nation's capital, Washington. This almost-in-jest suggestion was begun to be considered seriously by Wiley, as he knew that Dan had been in the New York State National Guard, and because of this, would make a perfect candidate to lead a unit. Dan thought that this was a fine idea if they could get authorization from the governor of New York, Edwin Morgan, and funds to start the procedure.

They were given the permission to recruit, and handbills were printed and distributed to all interested in joining. Recruiting speeches were delivered by Dan, who really knew how to talk and convince young men to volunteer. In short order they had raised a regiment of eight companies. The governor was delighted and gave Dan and Wiley orders to raise a full brigade of five regiments! Now Dan was in full swing and his good friend, Charles K. Graham, head of the Brooklyn Navy Yard, for whom Dan had procured the job, left with four hundred brawny naval yard workers who were eager to fight for the Union. Another young man who would join and become an important ally and friend to Dan all through the rest of his life, was a cleric from Connecticut, Joseph H. Twitchell. He, at first thought that Dan had not much promise, with his background, but he came to trust and admire this man who was to lead the corps of which Rev. Twitchell would be a chaplain.

Now there were three thousand enlistees as volunteers and they had to obtain a name, a title. How better than by using the inscription on the New York State seal, "Excelsior," than the Excelsior Brigade? When Governor Morgan heard of this formidable number from New York City alone, he could see that this would cause trouble in other sections of the state and telegraphed Dan to dismiss two thousand enlistees at once and send them home. Dan was furious! He had worked hard to form this brigade, and he smelled politics working against him, as the governor was a Republican and Dan had no political friends as such as this time.

Another consideration was affected by this plan, which rattled Dan. The rank of the officer heading the unit was dictated by the number of men enlisted. If a regiment of about one thousand men enlisted, the officer was a colonel, if he enlisted a brigade of twenty-five hundred men, the officer would become a one-star brigadier general. Being ordered to return to civilian life over two thousand enlistees, Dan would be reduced in rank to a colonel!

Dan took the earliest train to Washington to see President Lincoln. This was really their first face-to-face meeting, excepting for one right after Lincoln had been elected president and had come to Washington, to Willard's Hotel where the two of them had met briefly at a social function.

Now Dan had to make his plea for keeping all of the enlisted men he had worked so hard to sign up and planned to train for the Excelsior Brigade. His plan, which he proposed to Lincoln, was that if the union were to be kept, then the troops should be Federal troops, not just the state militia and state volunteers, as it now stood. He stressed that if New York State would not take all of the men he had enlisted, then the United States should, as volunteers. President Lincoln liked the idea but could see that it would interfere with the states procedures to raise troops. This might, and probably would, make enemies of many governors for a new president.

Dan's reply was that the "power to raise armies" had been granted to Congress. The president was persuaded by this forthright man who spoke so eloquently and intelligently, even for a Democrat. Lincoln was well aware of Dan's past troubles, but he was trying to hold out his hand of friendship to all Americans. Lincoln talked with Secretary of War Simon Cameron, who also saw merit in Dan's plan, and Sickles was told to keep the total of the men enlisted and wait, they would be accepted! "We will see how this beginning ends," was Lincoln's comment.[1]

While Dan was away on the business of recruiting of volunteers over the Fourth of July holiday, Teresa wrote to her oldest friend, Florence, of whom we know nothing, of her celebration in Bloomingdale. She had both of her parents there to help her celebrate. She wrote, "I cannot begin to tell you all the sport we had, went rowing, stilt walking, seesawing on the whirligig, pitching, quoits, racing, riding, eating and drinking out of doors. In the evening we had a fine display of fireworks and then a large bonfire. . . ." It was as though no war could be going on, nor mention of it or any indication of her husband's activities at the time.

"The next night," she continued, "I slapped Ma in the face, and she threw water on me, so pitcher after pitcher of water was thrown, and I got drenched, the hall looked like a small lake. I ran to get away from Ma when I slipped on the floor near the applewood room and down I went, hurt both of my arms and hands, as for my body, it is a mass of black and blue spots."

She added, "I have two new dogs. I am also to have two peacocks and a monkey, and what after that I do not know, not a baby, I promise you." This would imply that she and Dan had not been having sexual relations at that time or before. Dan wrote to Laura, who was now nearing nine years of age. She wrote to him as follows on one occasion.

> Mamma, Grand mamma, and I spent the day with Grandma Sickles, on Wednesday, and had a pleasant time.
>
> How very fine your soldiers and horses must appear and how glad I should be to see them. Will you let us come to see you one of these days? Grandma Sickles says she intends to make you a visit.
>
> Oh, how happy we shall be if you can come home to us at Christmas!
>
> Accept an affectionate embrace and 10,000 kisses dear, good Papa, from your Laura.[2]

He did not come home for Christmas, it is believed. . . .

Dan returned from Washington elated that his plan to keep all of his volunteers had been implemented and that they would be mustered out of New York State command to that of the United States. The New York politicians were livid that the president had decided to raise volunteers from the states directly, bypassing the political sanctums and possible graft of, in their minds, their rights. Letters and telegrams arrived on Lincoln's desk daily from all quarters. Other states felt threatened by this vast decision for change.

Dan had taken a chance stating his plan to the president, that he would undertake the cost of equipping the brigade himself. No mean task for several thousand men, supplying living quarters, food, arms, and ammunition, all equipment, uniforms, and pay them besides. He had been housing the men in some private homes and a New York State barracks as they arrived in New York City from their homes in the state, tired and disheveled. They had little to do and roamed the streets, some drinking, fighting, and upsetting the residents. Finally the police and the City Board of Health complained, and Dan had to work fast to relieve the tension. He found a bath house where for the cost of ten cents a man, they received a bath, shave, and a haircut, so at least they looked more presentable.[3]

Dan's quartermaster, his friend Wiley, had gotten two chefs who worked at Delmonico's to prepare the food! It was obvious that Dan had a large tiger by the tail! The cost of all of this exceeded $12,000 a week. . . . .

The politicians were doing everything they could to hamper and delay Dan's attempts to better the Excelsior Brigade. They were successful in closing down the state barracks, so Dan had to find other housing for the men at once. He solved that by buying a very large circus tent from P.T. Barnum, which was raised on vacant ground that he was able to use on Staten Island. Things were going from bad to worse as men kept arriving and others deserted daily. Some money was donated by patriotic citizens and organizations, but most of everything used was bought on credit and debt was mounting fast. Dan's father, whose patriotism was aflame, was using his own money to keep the momentum going.

Dan called the Staten Island location, Camp Scott, after the venerable General of the Army, Winfield Scott, and at last a real camp was established for the training of troops. Still, the final process of enlisting United States Volunteers had not been settled, and pressure was put on the president to accomplish this end. The food was spoiling for lack of refrigeration, meaning ice, the tent was not large enough to hold more arriving men, and many had to sleep on the ground. More and more men deserted as they had, "answered the call" and were mostly honest lads who wanted to join up, be trained, move South to fight, and get the war over as fast as possible. The glamour of the war had not arrived. They had only three hundred antiquated rifles, which they exchanged with each other during drill. Dan was working as hard as possible to make the venture work, as this was just the sort of problem he thrived on. Most of the men liked him and his spunk, and realized that he was working for them.

Sickles went again to see President Lincoln, who said, "Your camp has all gone to pieces, I hear." Dan said, "Not yet!" But things were precarious at this point, and firm plans for United States Volunteers had to be put in place, if it were not to fall into pieces. Lincoln told Dan to wait three more days and he "would take him out of the cold." Dan assumed that all would be well after that, but more trouble was approaching, as more men left than ever. They felt as though they had never been enlisted properly, as expected, could leave whenever they wished, and still not be called deserters.

No one was ever frustrated as Dan Sickles by roadblocks being used against him, and it was only his perseverance that succeeded. No salaries were being paid now and the men had to beg for money from their families for sundries for everyday living.

Rev. Twitchell was most impressed by Dan's insistence on a policy of no drinking and no fighting for the men. Finally two Army officers arrived and they swore in the men as United States Volunteers. . . . "On to Richmond" was the cry heard all over the camp.

The end of the problem was, however, not in sight still as for the two months that Dan had the men, the credit was exhausted and bills were coming due with alarming regularity. Legal judgments were secured against Dan to force the payment of monies before the soldiers were to leave, whenever that would be. Sickles was determined to lead his men into battle, and he was able to persuade the many creditors to be patient.

The first showdown battle occurred at Bull Run, or Manassas. The troops streamed back as fast as they were able to Washington, and a panic took over quickly. Three months had gone by when at last the Excelsior Brigade was put aboard trains on July 22, 1861, for Washington. Dan's old friend, Wiley, had had enough. His being left with the bills to pay from some unknown source, made for a parting of the ways with Sickles. They were, in time to get past this difficulty and regain their friendship with each other.

When the Excelsior Brigade arrived in Washington, they took the location in a meadow on the city perimeter, and started to train seriously to become a fighting force. After Bull Run,[4] both sides stood back to take stock of the battle that neither had been prepared to fight at the time. Lincoln said that both sides were "green," and he was correct. Calmer heads realized that it would take almost a year of gearing up by both North and South to become strong enough to bring the war to a swift conclusion, whichever way it could be ended.

Sickles was a provisional brigadier general now, earning $300 a month, and in command of five regiments. He

Brigadier General Daniel E. Sickles

was back, as near to Washington as could be expected, in a meadow, in good spirits, with his past troubles behind him, and he was headed in the right direction for success.

Dan sincerely thanked President Lincoln for his support during the dark days of the Excelsior's Brigade's earlier troubles gaining United States Volunteer status. Lincoln liked this strong man who used his wits and personality so well. His wife, Mary, also looked on Dan as a friend and welcomed him to the White House. They both were aware of the nature of Sickles's past life and political enemies who would never let him forget what was over, as far as Dan was concerned.

Dan's friend and former lawyer, Edwin Stanton, was now legal counsel to the Secretary of War, Simon Cameron, and the two of them were in contact at times. The old Stockton Mansion was a very short walk of one half a block from the White House, and I imagine that Dan, if he was in the vicinity, would have noticed the house and thought back two years or more to that part of his life, but I am sure that he did not dwell on that, as what was past was definitely past for Dan. After three months of more or less skillful training, the Excelsior Brigade moved to Maryland in October, on the Potomac River to join the division of Brigadier General Joseph Hooker. There would begin a long friendship that would last far past the war years. Hooker was a West Pointer, who like most of his fellow alumni from there, looked down with disdain on political generals, and this was true for Dan as well. They would have to come to some understanding and for a while, there was a three-way battle of temperaments between Sickles, Hooker, and General George B. McClellan, who now headed the Army of the Potomac.

Dan had had some military training, but he lacked the experience of actual fighting before now. Nevertheless he was a born leader, no doubt of that, if his men were questioned. He wrote letters to Laura, who termed what she received as "affectionate letters," but he did not correspond with Teresa as much as with his parents.

In December 1861, Governor Morgan of New York was able to change the policy and the Excelsior Brigade was incorporated back into the New York State troops. It could still recruit across the nation, but the First, Second, Third, Fourth, and Fifth U.S. Volunteers were changed into the Seventieth, Seventieth-first, Seventieth-second, Seventieth-third, and Seventieth-fourth New York State troops. This was a plan. The plan, to erase the name Excelsior Brigade, and perhaps Dan Sickles with it! He was returned to a colonelship and ousted from his command. Immediately he contacted Lincoln, Stanton, McClellan, and Hooker, and was restored to command after three months' time, with the rank of Brigadier General restored.

Ten
The Years of War

Here at last, Dan led his brigade at the Battle of Fair Oaks, against his enemy, General James Longstreet. Little did they both know then that one day the two of them would become close friends after the end of the Civil War, when they would meet again in Gettysburg, go over the ground together, and visit other places where they fought each other valiantly many times.

Dan Sickles's first taste of combat had been when he led a bayonet charge at the Battle of Fair Oaks, Virginia, on May 31st through June 1st, 1862.[1] The charge was not made because the troops were out of ammunition, as happened to Colonel Joshua Chamberlain at Gettysburg when the Twentieth Maine was upon Little Round Top, but when the opposing side sees men running towards them with the "cold steel" gleaming, there is fear enough to turn and run the opposite way. There were casualties, a great many at Fair Oaks, but Dan led his troops himself, and it was a difficult transition from being general to a general leading his own men into battle. The following is an excerpt from Dan Sickles himself of the experience.

> Early in 1862, before the Peninsular Campaign began, General McClellan was in Washington and somehow he lost track of a portion of the Confederate Army. General

Hooker, my commander, chose me to make a reconnaissance in force and try to uncover the position of General Longstreet. I took a thousand of my brigade and I picked them myself, taking the huskiest and most reliable I could find. We crossed the river from Maryland and made a march of some miles toward Fredericksburg at a place called Stafford Court House. We met the outpost of Longstreet's Army, two regiments in all. They outnumbered us two to one and it was a hot fight. It was the first time that I or any of my men had been under fire. I was surprised when it was over and the Confederates had retired, evidently thinking that we were the advance guard of the whole army.

Throughout the disastrous Manassas campaign under General Pope, Sickles's Excelsiors had been continually in action. At Bristoe, Groveton, Second Bull Run, and Chantilly, they had fought stubbornly, and suffered brutally. At the close of the campaign, they were found so shattered, depleted, and exhausted, that when the army under the reappointed McClellan marched to meet General Lee at Antietam, they were put on garrison duty at Alexandria to rest and recruit, and so for the first time since they took the field, they missed an important engagement. But two months later, they rejoined the Third Corps in charge of three brigades and a battery of artillery.

An interesting story was told about a Tammany friend of Dan's, who suggested that perhaps Teresa should visit the wounded of the Excelsior Brigades in 1862, who were then in New York City hospitals. She agreed at first, but soon gave more thought to the suggestion, until she could find out what the general wanted her to do.[2] She did not visit the wounded, so Dan must have written his opposition to the plan. There is no doubt in my mind that she would have made a fine showing at the hospital, and it probably would have done her much good to be a small part of the war effort. The men would have enjoyed her beauty and their being able to see their general's wife, but he must have felt differently about exposing her to any comment after so many years passing. I have never been sure that the American public ever knew that although the two of them were not divorced, they were separated in body and mind and always would remain so.

The two armies sat on opposite banks of the Potomac River biding time, with nothing happening. General McClellan had forged a great army, well trained, well fed, and well equipped, but heading nowhere! The president was questioning if McClellan wanted to fight at all! The men soon grew bored with this inaction, bickering among themselves, and finding ways to get whiskey.

There was fighting in the ranks instead of between Northerners and Southerners, and many officers were involved in the squabbling also. The division had moved eighteen miles down the Potomac River, and waited some more in the mud. Morale was lower than ever, broken only by the arrival of Thaddeus Lowe's gas balloon, which showed up for a trial run. General Hooker and Sickles watched the balloon inflate, showing a portrait of George Washington on one side. This was a true temptation to Sickles, and he went up several times to see and record enemy batteries on the Rebel side of the river. The general was attired in his well-tailored uniform, gleaming with insignia as the balloon lifted over the campfires.

Another piece of good news from Washington was the removal of Simon Cameron as President Lincoln's Secretary of War, and his being replaced by Sickles's friend, Edwin Stanton. Dan immediately renamed his camp, Camp Stanton.

Again fate and bad luck moved against Dan when Lincoln revoked his appointment as Brigadier General of Volunteers, so Hooker appointed Colonel Nelson Taylor to assume control of the Excelsior Brigades. Sickles sent a note to Hooker, reminding him that HE was the senior colonel of the brigade, and claimed the right to remain. He would obey the ruling, but he would appeal for redress to General McClellan. He got moral support from Charles K. Graham, who resigned his post in indignation.

President Lincoln told McClellan to move, an order not to be disobeyed this time, and now that the army was to move at last, Dan was not in it, as he had written a farewell to his soldiers, gone to Washington, determined to redeem himself with every effort involving anyone who could help him. All of his friends were contacted for help against the bloc of enemies who stood in his way. To the world, "General Sickles is at Willard's," a Washington paper explained. While Dan was in town, his friend, Thomas Francis Meagher, was unanimously voted by the Senate as a brigadier general. Dan pulled every string he knew to have Lincoln renominate him, if he could be sure of their confirmation. His father, George, wrote him, "I know that the Republican party could not act towards you as you have towards the nation. . . . To me it seems cruel that you should be willing to sacrifice everything, even life itself and be refused the poor privilege by a set of driveling apes."[3]

New York newspaper editors, such as Horace Greeley and William Cullen Bryant, circulated petitions seeking Sickles's renomination. The former hatred between these men and Sickles had softened to gentleness from them. Unbelievable! His friends knew the general's weaknesses, but his vast strength was never forgotten by them either.

The men of the Excelsior Brigade were elated when news of their commander's confirmation was known. Sickles was able, whatever his other failures, to inspire with real affection the camaraderie of obedience and respect that can only be brought out by someone born to lead.

General McClellan, meanwhile, had advanced to Fortress Monroe, on the Peninsula and was moving towards Richmond. The two sides clashed at Williamsburg, Virginia, and the Rebels retreated towards Richmond. The Excelsior Brigade lost 772 men under the leadership of Colonel Taylor. Dan returned to find his brigade, now known as the Second Brigade of Hooker's Division of the Third Army Corps, led by the older General Samuel Heintzelman. He was warmly received by his men, who by now had tasted the bitter wine of war, fully realizing how their army life had changed after burying comrades on Southern ground.

Here, before Richmond, Dan came to know the officers who would later have a strong impact on his future, such as George Gordon Meade, Daniel Butterfield, and Oliver Otis Howard. He also came to know three Frenchmen of royal blood who had been exiled by Napoleon III and had joined General McClellan's staff. Prince de Joinville and his two nephews, the Compte de Paris, the pretender to the throne of France, and the Duc de Chartes. Dan's knowledge of the French language was a real plus in their friendship, and they got along famously. Sooner or later, Dan's knowledge of so much he had learned through the years of diplomacy, language, and leadership were coming through to his great advantage.

So sat the Army of the Potomac, less than twenty miles from Richmond, mainly because General McClellan mistakenly believed that there were far more troops than there actually were. At this time, Dan's friends, the royal Frenchmen, left for Europe to return to exile at another location.

The waiting was softened by parties given by Generals Hooker, Sickles, and Butterfield. These parties were criticized by the press as brothels and barroom excuses for debauchment, but they served the purpose of breaking the solemn period of boredom, combined with war weariness.[4]

Sickles got leave to go to New York to recruit new men, as his own brigade had a loss of 2,500 casualties, and it was more difficult to enlist volunteers when the public could see a longer, and more costly in lives, war. The three months enlistment had been fulfilled and as men left for home, it was harder to find others to take their places without hard campaigning, a task Sickles could do with ease. His leave was not to be given routinely to commanders, but was ordered only when gaining new recruits was absolutely necessary. Also having influence with Secretary of War Stanton did not hurt. Dan, along with General Meagher, whose Irish Brigade was also in need of more recruits, left for New York in July 1862.

Dan, helped by Chaplain Twichell, who had been given a leave, and many wounded Excelsior's furloughed men, gave a rally at the Seventh Regiment Armory in New York City, where the general talked for an hour or more to the city's volunteer firemen. He made trips to upstate New York to speak and recruit there. He knew how to speak well, and while many of the West Point graduates were good officers, speaking was not one of their courses and they could never deliver any important message. Dan knew what he believed and was not afraid to say it. The war, he said, was aimed only at putting down a rebellion against civil authority and an established government. This recruitment drive lasted two months.

General McClellan had failed with the Peninsula Campaign. Lincoln relieved McClellan and appointed General John Pope, who himself lasted only a short time after being defeated at Second Bull Run by Generals Lee and Jackson. Major General Henry Wager Hallock was then installed, and he also did not last, so in desperation, Lincoln reinstated General McClellan, having no other general to command the army.

When Dan Sickles left, he would not know his absence would fall so heavily on the men who were left to fight. General Hooker was a corps commander with the returned McClellan, and so Dan was also elevated to Hooker's old division, to be made a Major General, the highest Union Army rank at that time.

Antietam gave the Union Army control of the battlefield after an attack that crushed the Confederate spearhead. This proved to be the bloodiest conflict of the war so far. General McClellan could have turned the tide of Union losses and perhaps ended the conflict then, but again he procrastinated, and Lincoln was thwarted as usual by his general. The president tried again by appointing General Ambrose Burnside, a well-liked, honest, and devoted to the Union man, who revised the army into three "Grand Divisions" commanded by Generals Hooker, Sumner, and W.B. Franklin, each having two army corps in each division.

Dan received his Major General status and a salary of $445 a month, which would help him sustain his lifestyle. The three generals' troops were overwhelmed at Fredericksburg with terrible losses, but Sickles's men were held in reserve and here spent two more days after the worst of the fighting had taken place with the corps of General James Longstreet.

President Lincoln then replaced Burnside, whom he liked, with Joseph Hooker, whom he liked less. The generals were moving in and out too rapidly to be tracked easily. . . . .

The Old Excelsior Brigade was now led by Brigadier Joseph Revere, from New Jersey, and the grandson of Paul Revere, the patriot. The general was offered the hospitality of his Division Commander, Dan Sickles, on New Year's Day, 1863. Here was all manner of fine food, drink, and music. There was too much liquor here for Rev. Twichell, and the Catholic Father O'Hagan, who left together after a short visit.

The weather was bad that winter of 1863, and camp life was boring and bitter cold with the Federals at Falmouth, Virginia, and the Confederates across the Potomac at Fredericksburg. A soldier's truce was worked out between the opposite sides for pickets, allowing no unnecessary firing, and even some trading in small pleasures of life, such as coffee and tobacco took place between the forces waiting out the winter.

General Hooker gave up the Three Grand Divisions and recognized the Army of the Potomac into the former corps. General John Reynolds headed the First Corps; General Darius Couch, the Second Corps; General Daniel Sickles, the Third Corps; General George Meade, the Fifth Corps; General John Sedgwick, the Sixth Corps; General Franz Sigel, the Eleventh Corps; General Henry Slocum, the Twelfth Corps. The only non-West Point men were generals Sigel and Sickles.

General Sigel resigned by choice, and General Oliver O. Howard was appointed to command the Eleventh Corps. For Hooker's Chief of Staff, he chose a non-West Pointer, Daniel Butterfield, of New York, who had fought well under McClellan, Pope, and Burnside. His most notable contribution was composing bugle calls, and especially what we now call "Taps," a call originally meant to denote the end of the soldier's day, played at evening when they retired. It was a comforting sound when all was quiet and the notes rang over the stillness of the camp. It was fondly recalled by the men who heard it and were glad to still be there to hear it again.

General Meade, commanding the Fifth Corps, did not find either Sickles or Butterfield to his liking, as he believed that they were opportunists, each being more clever than Hooker. The men in the ranks, however, liked both men as they were not aware of the wrangling that permeated the upper crust of the army's command, and really did not care unless the action reached down to them. At this time, Butterfield originated the idea of a patch for each of the corps, a red diamond on a white ground for the Third Corps of Sickles, a trefoil for the Second Corps, the triangle for the Fourth Corps, the Maltese Cross for the Fifth Corps, the Greek Cross for the Sixth Corps, a crescent for the Eleventh Corps, and a star for the Twelfth Corps. These badges were cut out of flannel for hats or could have been of metal with a pin on the back. The men liked the idea of identifying their corps and were proud of attaching them to their hats.

During this change of command after Hooker's promotion, the army worked hard drilling and making a snug winter encampment. Boredom was overcome with a supply of officers' wives who joined their husbands for some time during the winter. There was entertainment and dancing. Some of the straight-laced officials, who were aghast at this sort of thing taking place, went on record about Hooker's army site as a combination "bar room and brothel." There was always someone out to still the fun! Even Delmonico's arrived with fine foods, and chefs, and everything needed for sumptuous parties for many hundreds of persons. The "Padres" were not present as they were aware of much drinking that would be taking place. Commander Sickles did himself proud. Not only the officers had a fine time, the men had festive occasions also such as horse races, games, and marksmanship competition. Saint Patrick's Day was also celebrated, especially by the Irish of General Meagher's Irish Brigade.

President Lincoln, trusting in God and General Hooker to deliver him from the steady progression of leaders who would not or could not lead, arrived in the winter camp to be feted, along with Mrs. Lincoln. It was truly a grand affair.

The Picnic—July 1862

This delightful story, told by Daniel Sickles, in his own words at a speech before the Society of the Army of the Potomac in the year 1912:

> In the thick of the Peninsula Campaign, at Malvern Hill, to be exact, I had the occasion to employ a section of artillery, and hunting up my division commander, General Joe Hooker, I asked him if I could detach a couple of guns for use in my brigade.
>
> "Fighting Joe," however, seemed to have his mind on something else. "Guns? Guns?" he snorted. "Oh, yes, you can have guns or anything else you want if you will only give me something to eat. I am starving!" I dug in my pocket and pulled out a chunk of hardtack and a small bag of brown sugar. Hooker stared at me in amazement. "If you will tell me where you find sugar and hardtack, you can have four guns! If only you will do this, you can have a whole damned battery!" I said, "General, if you send an orderly a few miles back along the road I have just come, he will find a broken-down wagon of the commissary train loaded with sugar and army biscuit. That is where I got this." Hooker bawled for his orderly, and I rode off with my guns!

The next morning, the army had reached Harrison's Landing. It was July and terribly hot. But I was in high spirits, and for a very good reason! I hurried over to the headquarter's tent and found General Heintzelman, my corps commander, Generals Kearny, Hooker, and Warren, and my two good friends, the French military attachés, the Compte de Paris, and his brother, the Duc de Chartes, busy over maps and reports.

"Gentlemen, I said, "Would you do me the honor to lunch with me at my camp?" Heintzelman squinted up from a chart he was studying. "None of your jokes, Sickles! You know you have nothing but sugar and biscuit."

Blandly I countered, "Come and see!" There were about twenty staff officers present, and raising my voice a little, I cried, "Gentlemen, lunch is laid out and waiting, won't you do me the honor? Twenty pairs of incredulous eyes were staring at me. There was a general murmuring suggestive of what would be done to me if I were merely fooling with empty bellies. But, at last, hesitantly, the whole group followed me.

My camp happened to be pitched in a charming spot, a small grove by the riverbank, with a fine natural lawn. When my guests arrived, they saw, to their wild surprise, a huge white cloth spread out on the turf, punctiliously set with white porcelain plates and dishes, napkins, polished knives and forks, wineglasses, and all the appointments of a luxurious dinner table.

"The rascal has robbed a hotel!" cried Hooker. Kearny was skeptical. "There are no hotels around here, General, that's plantation loot!" At that moment, as I had given directions, my orderlies appeared bearing two large pails, one of purple, the other of amber liquid, both garnished with lumps of ice, fresh strawberries, sliced oranges, pineapples, and lemons, a most potent punch. Kearny seized one pail, Hooker the other, both dropping on their knees, as if in adoration. And while one grasped a chunk of ice and kissed it, the other squatted before his pail and drank from the brim like an Arab in the desert. Meanwhile, my orderlies reappeared with great platters of roast turkey and chicken, steaming rounds of beef, hams, fresh vegetables and fruits, and even cranberry sauce! Never was a man so bedeviled with questions as I was. But I remained mysterious. When Hooker cried, "But this is all a dream, Sickles," I replied, "It is, General, and I advise you to finish the turkey before you wake up!" But as first hunger was appeased and the good punch warmed us all, I confessed, "The truth is gentlemen, that early this morning a steamboat arrived at the landing laden with every luxury from the northern markets for the sick and wounded of the army, a gift from that good angel of mercy, the Sanitary Commission. The agent in charge applied to me for wagons and men to transport the supplies to our hospital camps, and I promptly complied, requesting, however, that one wagonload be granted to my famishing headquarters staff. My request was granted with a smile. And that wagonload was a royal one, you will grant! My orderlies did the rest. So gentlemen, a toast, The Sanitary Commission![5]

After Fredericksburg, the Army of the Potomac was demoralized by the failure to win over the Rebels even with their superior forces. General Hooker's plan for his 120,000-man army, and General Lee with almost half of that number against the Federal forces, was to turn General Sedgwick's large Sixth Corps across the Rappahannock River near Fredericksburg, keeping Sickles's Third Corps and Reynolds's First in reserve. As usual, there were wrong assumptions made as General Hooker was the only one aware of his planned assault. There was much confusion, as Hooker, who had riled against McClellan's slow tactics and the very same with Burnside, was now exhibiting the defensive posture of his predecessors. Hooker's order to fall back was received in disbelief by his generals. Meanwhile, Stonewall Jackson's 30,000 men were moving around the Federal troops, to attack them from the west.

Sickles was at Hazel Grove awaiting orders from Hooker, who arrived to look over the position. Sickles wanted to stay, but Hooker ordered him to withdraw and link up with the main force at Chancellorsville. Finally Hooker devised a plan, which if realized, was as much a decision of the true Napoleonic tactics as possible. The plan was comprised of using three corps against Fredericksburg and to sweep the flank, with the remaining four corps across the Rappahannock and Rapidan rivers, taking the enemy in reverse and enclosing vise-like jaws to crush him. The cavalry was ordered to cut off Lee's supply lines to Richmond. The generals of the army, surprised and encouraged by Hooker's near-clever tactical strategy, moved their huge wagon trains with purpose, hoping that perhaps these moves would bring victory within their grasp. The corps were positioned and General Stoneman and twelve thousand cavalry troops made a sweeping curve to raid Lee's communications with Richmond.

That fateful night, General Jackson was out in the dark woods, lighted by a full moon. He had warned his troops that the Union forces were also roaming the woods, and to keep a sharp eye out for them. His troops took his warning seriously and when horsemen were there, not knowing really if they were indeed Union forces also roaming the woods, but suspecting they were, they fired on Jackson's staff hitting their leader, seriously wounding him. The Confederate command was turned over to Jeb Stuart, who led the cavalry. Because of Jackson's wounding, the Rebels were incensed and threw themselves into the fury with shouts of, "Remember Jackson!" as they attacked Sickles's Third Corps with much loss of life to the Federal troops.

Hooker was filled with disbelief as his master plan had gone awry, although he had not allowed the two corps of Meade and Reynolds to come to Sickles's aid. Hooker took the responsibility of ordering a retirement from Chancellorsville, and so the Army of the Potomac left its position against smaller Confederate forces, and retreated across the Rappahannock River.

From Lincoln on down, fell the burden of explaining the fiasco at Chancellorsville to the country, and the editorials from the press condemned the leadership again. Sickles had lost 4,119 men, the largest number from any corps. Sickles was lauded in the papers by editors who had once vilified him, and he was noted as a soldier who showed skillfulness in battle. Dan felt reservations about leading an army, however, if it ever came to that. Hooker was still his good friend, even though he disagreed with his plans of order, and could rely on Dan standing by him.

General Meagher's command of the Irish Brigade had his forces reduced to four hundred men and he wanted to go home and recruit again, writing to Stanton for permission. He was not answered, and resigned at once! The draft was now in operation, but starting up slowly, with some problems in instituting the new system.

President Lincoln was troubled by having to decide whether he should again look for a new commander for the army, and face the wrath of a country already disgusted by the steady progression of generals, "passing through" after each loss of a battle, and decided to stay with Hooker, for the present anyway.

The Federal Army did not have too long to wait for further developments. While Dan was in New York for a short leave, the Confederate Army of Northern Virginia was on the move with a plan to take the war across the North-South borders and fight on the North's land.

There was one happening pertaining to Dan Sickles. One of his brigade commanders of his old Excelsior Brigade was Brigadier General Joseph Revere, grandson of the patriot, Paul Revere. When Major General Hiram Berry was killed at Chancellorsville, although the command should have gone to Brigadier General Joseph B. Carr, Revere led the men to the rear, as he believed that no man could have stood through such an onslaught. Revere's fellow Brigadier General, Gershom Mott, had been wounded and so Revere took it upon himself to leave the field, when the men protested as well, that they should not. This was done without the knowledge of Sickles, his Corps Commander. Because of this the two brigades were "driven in." Revere was brought up on charges and a court marshall was convened at Third Corps Headquarters on the 12th of June, 1863 to try Brigadier General Joseph W. Revere on charges of "misbehavior before the enemy and neglect of duty." A distinguished court was assembled with General Winfield Scott Hancock, as president, and Generals Newton, Wadsworth, Humpheys, Gibbon, and Barlow, among the members. General David Birney acted as Revere's counsel. It was an important happening. General Daniel Sickles, General Revere's Corps Commander, testified bitterly against the man who marched the "Old Hooker Division" off the field without orders. Sickles cared most about the Excelsior Brigade as he always had since originating it in 1861, and he could not let the occurrence go without protest. After three days of testimony, General Revere was found guilty of "Conduct to the prejudice of good order and military discipline," and was sentenced to be dismissed from the service. General Hooker immediately approved the verdict. Later the verdict was revoked by President Lincoln in view of Revere's previous good record, on September 10, 1864. His voluntary resignation was accepted by Lincoln from August 1863.[6]

It was reported that Dan Sickles was wounded slightly at Chancellorsville when a spent shot or piece of shell stuck his waist belt, and he was hospitalized for a short time, returning to duty before the Battle of Gettysburg.

President Lincoln could see that another important fight was to occur in the near future, and that it was time to consider replacing Hooker with another general, although he sincerely wished that it would not be necessary. His choice was General George G. Meade, who was not delighted to hear the news that he was being ordered to lead the Army of the Potomac. He wrote to his wife, he could not refuse. . . . Hooker's plans were not used and he resigned.

Sickles rejoined the army at Frederick, Maryland, the day that Hooker resigned. He realized that his relations with General Meade would not be the same as with Hooker, and conditions would be less personal, as Meade was quarrelsome, knowing of Sickles's preference for Hooker.

The two armies marched north in June 1863, keeping their distance from each other, knowing that a larger battle would be coming soon, when they at last were to meet. They were heading toward a small town that no one had heard of—Gettysburg, Pennsylvania.

Lee was flushed with victory, again and again, and thought that the next confrontation would prove to be another. He quietly approached Chambersburg, to be his temporary headquarters. He also permitted Jeb Stuart to take his entire cavalry off on a raid around the Federal forces, but leaving the Army of Northern Virginia without knowledge of where the Union troops were going and the numbers of men included. Time was fleeting and both sides knew it. . . . Lee was overconfident this time after several good results from his decisions, and being on Northern soil had a heady effect on him.

Since studying the Civil War, it is my considered opinion that to be a general then, or really in any way where thousands of troops are moved according to plans devised for them, is probably one of the most difficult positions in which one can be found. As a general-in-chief, your plan may seem perfect to you, but it is only your plan, and the enemy's also must be considered. He is thinking the same of his plans and two sides must deal with weather conditions, heavy rains, flooding rivers to be crossed that were lower when planned before, mud that bogs down troops, wagons, and cannons. No wonder so many of the leading generals fell in esteem, as one by one of the Army of the Potomac commanders arrived with enthusiasm and left with defeat. Perhaps if Generals Grant and Sherman had been singled out for command after Fredericksburg and Chancellorsville, the tide might have turned earlier.

The officers of the army were strange men to each other. Sometimes "the enemy" were men of their own army who made mistakes, not the opposing side. In addition, it seems that some men were more or less pious, had fine marriages and families, and were sober, but some were not. Hooker, Butterfield, and Sickles were considered the "other end of commanders," rightly or wrongly. People are different. . . . Hooker never married and sought out women, which is natural, along with Sickles, who although married, was not really married as far as his life was concerned, after the affair and trial and his even placing Teresa back in the home, sought out women also. Daniel Butterfield was married, although later in life, but not much has been written about his personal life. My point is that judgments are made about personal lives so easily. A good leader of men should be judged on other personal traits of command more than the above mentioned.

Whatever is said of George Meade, he was not flamboyant, but had solid commands and the respect of most of his fellow officers. Each general before him had had a trial by fire and Meade was to join the cadre.

Sickles had learned a lesson at Chancellorsville, and that was to use his own intuition to take advantage of opportunities when they appeared on his own ground, and then put trust in headquarters to back him up. With this purpose, he marched back to Falmouth, under Hooker, to await the next move by either army.

The town of Gettysburg had not been intended as a location for a battle. General Lee had envisioned Cashtown, Pennsylvania, for his meeting, and General Meade had settled on a meeting at Pipe Creek, to cover Baltimore and Washington, about thirty miles away to the South.

A large detachment of Confederates made its way into Gettysburg, reportedly looking for needed shoes for its barefoot men. General John Buford arrived in Gettysburg with his cavalry to find the Rebels indeed arriving, and he made his decision to hold there with his two brigades of about twenty-five hundred men. This was his decision alone and it proves that such judgments are to be desired, a firmness that becomes necessary in decision and obvious to one man, a commander. It is considered a good quality, and especially by a general who is out to win during a war. Putting oneself "on the line" is hailed if successful. . . .

General Meade had ordered General John Fulton Reynolds and his First Corps to move towards Gettysburg with General Howard's Eleventh Corps, with Sickles's Third Corps to protect the rear and flanks. Meade had Sickles at Emmitsburg, about ten miles from Gettysburg to see if there would be a good place for a fight, but Reynolds wired for Sickles, his nearest subordinate commander, to come to Gettysburg at once to help. Sickles had no time to consult with Meade, and leaving two brigades behind to hold Emmitsburg, he left with his troops, wiring Meade for support or recall. Meade agreed with his decision to support Reynolds, so the two brigades were moved to join the rest of the army corps.

In the spring of 1863, the foundation was laid for the Third Corps Union, an organization that was unique to the army. This group formed was to help the officers of the corps with any problems that they themselves could not solve. If there was an injury or death, the man's family was helped with funds that the men contributed to themselves. Burials were arranged after embalming, the bodies identified and returned to the families. This process was deeply appreciated by the men, to be so cared for by their commanders.

On June 28th, 1863, General Sickles resumed command of the Third Corps, after being away for several weeks.[7] In his absence, the commander of the Third Corps was General David Bell Birney. He said that he was glad to see Sickles back as the responsibilities of a command like that, to a temporary commander, were very great. Generals Sickles and Birney were good friends, and both commanders. General Birney was commander of the First Division of the Third Corps, and as such was an important part of the corps, backing Sickles, and the two worked together well. They were united in an esprit de corps among their men, which made the corps celebrated for the feeling of unity that existed.

General Birney contracted malaria before Richmond. Although he had spent three and a half years without a severe wound, he died on October 18, 1864. He was thirty-nine years old with a wife, Antoinette, and six little children, five of whom attended the funeral, the smallest just an infant. Birney was a favorite son of Pennsylvania, and so laid in state at Independence Hall. General Sickles was at the funeral, as the superior of General Birney in more than one bloody battle, testifying by his presence with his own mutilated body, his sense of the high and soldierly ability that distinguished the lamented deceased, and how profoundly he mourned the loss of a brother soldier. A $30,000 trust fund was set up by the members of the Third Corps Union to support Birney's wife and children. Attending the funeral were Generals Hooker, Sherman, Grant, Farragut, Sheridan, and Sickles.[8]

The ground had been decided. General Reynolds had been killed almost as soon as he had arrived on the field, by a Confederate bullet in the back of his neck, early in the morning of July 1st, 1863. General Abner Doubleday took command at once and carried on until Meade appointed General Winfield Scott Hancock as commanding general. Hancock could see how important Cemetery Ridge was to be, building up a five-mile course between that point and the two hills, "Sugar Loaf," which we call today Big Round Top, and "The Little Rocky Hill," known today as Little Round Top. This was the high ground desired by all commanders.

General Lee had his "Old War Horse," General James Longstreet, at his side, but surely missed the information that his head of cavalry, General Jeb Stuart, could have provided, wherever it was he could be found at this time. General Lee had allowed him to leave on a ride around the Army of the Potomac, but did not expect that he would not be in contact to reveal any movements that were necessary for the Army of Northern Virginia to plan this battle formation.

Dan Sickles had arrived in Gettysburg after the march with his men, and he headed toward the gatehouse at the

Gettysburg cemetery to await the arrival of General Meade. He met Generals Slocum and Howard there. This unusual structure consisted of two stories of red brick, one on each side of the cemetery's entrance road. There were two rooms, one up, and one down, with a kitchen and a cellar. The caretaker of the cemetery, Peter Thorn, had entered the Union Army and his wife, Catherine, was the caretaker in his absence.

Catherine Thorn had had an eventful day. She had baked six loaves of bread, which she gave to the soldiers and had pumped water from the well for them. A soldier approached and asked her if she would make supper for General Howard, General Slocum, and General Sickles. She had no bread but would make some "cakes." She went to a neighbor to get some more meat, as there was very little left, and found the house filled with wounded men from the day's fighting, six of whom "did not move." She returned to the gatehouse without the meat. While she was gone, the gatehouse had begun to fill with wounded soldiers also, and some were lying on her kitchen floor.

The cemetery gatehouse, no common hostelry, had some distinguished visitors that evening. Generals Howard, Slocum, and Sickles came to eat. In spite of having wounded men in her kitchen, Mrs. Thorn, served them two good-sized dough cakes, three pieces of meat, and coffee. General Howard had not eaten since the morning, was famished, and never forgot the meal. When the generals started to leave, she asked them if she should stay in the house. General Howard said, "Leave the house? Leave the house? Comrades, I say stay." Mrs. Thorn busied herself until 4:00 A.M., and then she went into the cellar and found seventeen people already there!

Mrs. Thorn was pregnant at this time, and she and her father buried a total of more than one hundred Union and

Confederate dead in the cemetery after the Battle of Gettysburg, as they could find no help with the task. This sort of thing was indeed remarkable for two people who were not up to the physical exertion of such an undertaking.

Dan Sickles's headquarters was set up at the Abraham Trostle farm in a field across from the farmhouse. His tent was by a large white oak tree, which is still there and still providing seedlings for the world as a "Witness Tree" from Gettysburg to be planted anywhere one would grow.

If Sickles got any sleep that night in the tent with such a day's work ahead promised for the morning, it was a miracle. But by 8:00, General Meade's aides arrived to see how the corps was faring. By then, Sickles was asleep but was awakened. One of the aides was General Meade's son, who went back to his father's headquarters nearby to inform him that Sickles was not sure just where he should go. Meade then sent his son back to tell Dan where he should be posted. To prolong the line along the ridge, already formed by the Second Corps. He was placed to the right of the Second Corp's left, extending his line to Little Round Top.

Sickles's Corps had two divisions, one commanded by General David Bell Birney, and the other by General Andrew Atkinson Humphreys. The morale was high and the men were ready to fight for them anywhere. General Humphreys was a West Pointer and a friend of Meade's, who knew of his commander's misgivings about Sickles, but did not show any outward signs of unfriendliness. General Meade was hesitant and cautious, but nevertheless was resolved to strengthen his backbone to rise to the occasion of total command about to commence.

General Meade had been awake most of the night of July 1st. Arriving so late there was no daylight left to see where he was and where the various units were temporarily encamped, he made his plans for posting the corps, a formidable job. General Slocum and the Twelfth Corps were on Culp's Hill. Cemetery Hill was covered by war-weary remnants of the First and Eleventh Corps. In between were the round top hills. The one called Big Round Top was seven hundred and fifty feet in height, Little Round Top being one hundred feet less, heavily treed in the rear, and not suitable for use in a battle. The front side had been felled by trees by its owner not too long before, and could be used by artillery to defend the area. The part of the ridge near Little Round Top was not as high as the rest and was not so easily defended. This was the section that Sickles was ordered to occupy.

Sickles was told to throw his men into a line from the Round Tops northward cross a stretch of lower ground until his right flank linked with the left of Hancock's Second Corps on Cemetery Ridge. Sickles had seen the terrain as too low to be of service, and he knew that the higher ground would be a far superior location. Meade had told him that he could use his own judgment as long as it was within the guidelines of his instruction. One half mile ahead was a higher ground, which would offer more protection. It was crowned by a peach orchard eight hundred yards in front of his assigned position. He then rode off to Meade's headquarters to get approval. Sickles was pleading his point with General Meade at the same time that General Hunt, Meade's artillery commander, had been making a check of the Federal artillery position. Hunt believed that he was in command of the field pieces, not Meade. . . . .

Meade told Hunt to inspect the line that Sickles had occupied with his Third Corps. Hunt, thereupon rode out with Sickles to the Peach Orchard and saw that Sickles had a point, even though the new position created a sharp salient. Hunt said that if such a line was held by sufficient strength and tied to the Round Tops on the left and to Hancock's Second Corps on the right, it would be acceptable. He knew that the Third Corps alone was not strong enough to man such a front and he probably questioned whether Meade had enough troops to reinforce Sickles adequately, when heavy gunfire was heard to the north and Hunt felt that he must return to army headquarters. As he turned to leave, Sickles asked whether the Third Corps should be moved out to the new line. "Not on my authority," but Hunt agreed to acquaint Meade with the layout.

Sickles was trying everything he could to have approval for the better position he had chosen before the battle started. General Meade had not given precise enough instructions in this matter. Perhaps he was not as familiar with the exact locations well enough during the short time he was on the field at Gettysburg. Sickles, on the other hand, had faced a similar situation in Chancellorsville when he was placed well and was ordered to vacate the ground. Against better judgment, he did leave and the Battle of Chancellorsville was lost. This he remembered. There was no thought of "Glory to be gained," only the realization that again the Army of the Potomac would more than likely suffer another defeat unless every base could be covered as well as possible. War is taking chances!

By now the Army of the Potomac troops, most of whom had marched for two days without sleep to meet at Gettysburg, without food, and adequate water in the intense heat of the July, had been posted in the famous fishhook configuration, with an open-ended horseshoe position on Cemetery Ridge.

At 3:00 A.M., Sickles advanced his ten-thousand-man Third Corps to the Emmitsburg Road. General Meade, unaware of Sickles's redeployment, summoned his corps commanders to a war council. Sickles sent word that he was too busy to attend. He was ordered to come, and did until heavy shelling to the south was heard. Meade had neglected his left wing all day and reacted quickly to battle sounds from that sector.

Sickles's artillery chief, Captain George E. Randolph, was delighted to get his guns to higher ground. General Hunt returned and Randolph came over and asked Hunt's approval of some gun locations suggested by Sickles. Dismounting, the two officers walked to the position. Hunt looked over the ground and said that if Sickles had ordered guns placed in the general area, the spot was as good as he could find. However, Hunt thought that Randolph did not have enough firepower in the Third Corps artillery to cover the front properly. To make up the shortage, Hunt sent to General Tyler and requested two batteries or twelve cannon, one of Napoleons, one of rifles. More could come from the reserve if needed.

There is an aura of battle. Amid the sounds of axes felling trees, of metal clashing, and the indescribable hum of thousands of muffled voices. Even louder words of command over the din. There is no time for any experience but the thought of preparation for battle. But when the preparations are made and men stand at rest, sweating in their heavy woolen uniforms, ready for action and the hours pass and nothing happens, a strange weird sensation takes possession of them. A mixed feeling with which deadly combat is awaited, neither pleasure or pain but a strangely blended mixture from knowing that the waiting and tension will soon be relieved by quick action upon receiving orders to move out. The mysterious unknown of life and death grips each man, until they are given orders to move at last into what they do not know, and try not to dwell on too much.

The battle raged, as Longstreet's men poured into the federal positions, the Wheatfield changing hands six times, the losses terrible, as the Peach Orchard was overrun. As the sun sunk lower in the Western sky, Sickles's reenforced salient was finally flattened and bent back to where the original position had been planned. The Southern hope had died, along with thousands of men. The smoke of many guns, the battle fog, remained in the still hot evening for a long while. The general still rode back and forth along his front, unhurt all day, until that moment when his life would change dramatically, in an instant.

Daniel Sickles made his own judgment to move to Gettysburg from Emmitsburg, Maryland, with a quick call from General Reynolds, to come at once. This was a soldierly act for which nothing but commendation had been given to him. Although the Third Corps lost heavily in the exposed position to which it had been moved, it did much to shatter the awful Confederate assaults thrown against it by Longstreet, preventing his troops from reaching the Union's main line. Although disastrous in some respects, the movement resulted in the enemy wasting all of its strength in gaining the Emmitsburg Road. An officer of General Humphrey's staff, who saw the fury of the fighting along the Emmitsburg Road, and who became one of the most careful scholars of the battle, believed that if General Sickles had NOT moved forward, Longstreet would have broken the main Federal line and would have reached the Taneytown Road, a view that Longstreet expressed himself in a letter to General Sickles.

It is also stated that General Meade paid insufficient attention to Sickles's reports about his position. Again, there should, have been explicit written orders with a plan from General Meade. It must be remembered that all armies are led by fallible egos and the blind fantasies of men. . . . . It still is and always will be so.

This is an excerpt from *Fighting for The Confederacy,* by General E. Porter Alexander, Chief of Artillery for the Army of Northern Virginia, First Division, under General James Longstreet as follows:

> General Sickles's Corps, by a misconception of orders, had taken position along this ridge, instead of the main shank. Along this ridge ran the Emmitsburg Pike. Sickles formed along this pike until he reached a crossroad, and then turned off to the left and rested his flank in some broken ground in the foot of Little Round Top. Neither Big or Little Round Top was occupied except for perhaps some pickets and a signal station. Meade did not like Sickles's position and was just about to bring him back to the shank line, as I may call it when our attack began. While on the subject, I may say, in my judgment, it was no harm to Meade to have our charge extend its first fury upon an advance line in front, where the shank line in rear gave such fine opportunity for artillery to cover the retreat of troops from the front. And Sickles claims that his advance position is what gave Meade the victory, and in my opinion, he has reasonable ground for thinking so.

The fate of General Sickles created a lot of interest among those who fought at Gettysburg, as he did survive the ordeal of being wounded, taken off the field, and transported back to care in Washington, D.C.

General Meade's report stated that Sickles had "not fully apprehended his instructions about the position to be taken, had advanced."

General Halleck wrote in his report that Sickles had misinterpreted his orders. Instead of placing the Third

The wounded General Sickles soon after the Battle of Gettysburg claimed his right leg in 1863.

Corps in a position to make it lie prolonged, he had moved it nearly three quarters of a mile in advance, an error that nearly proved fatal in battle.

The wording of these reports does not suggest that there was a desire to court-martial Sickles, as to do so would have been impractical and counterproductive and would have produced an awful row with President Lincoln. Sickles's wound had removed him from command of the Third Corps and that solved the immediate problem. Better to leave well enough alone was the decision.

Dan Sickles used efforts to unseat General Meade with the support of many officers, but he was not successful and he would never command his loved corps again.

Sickles campaigned all of the rest of his life for vindication of his actions on July 2, 1863, and George Meade never responded to any article or speech by General Sickles.

Eleven

Rebuilding the Union; the Reconstruction Period

Dan had recuperated quickly, mostly out of determination to lead his men again. Other commanders had been able to do this even with such a wounding, and he knew that. The men of the Third Corps wanted him back, and he was determined to prove that he could rise to the task if given the chance. For five months he wrote copious letters to anyone who could help him, especially President Lincoln, requesting to be "put back to work" for the union. He arrived in Washington on crutches, which he preferred, and started his efforts in person, giving up letter writing to persuade.

After Lincoln issued his Emancipation Proclamation and Amnesty Proclamation to the Confederate forces, they would receive pardon if they swore allegiance and certify that ten percent of its voting population had taken the oath. Ten weeks went by and there was still no reaction to the gesture of reconciliation. This troubled Lincoln and he realized that Dan Sickles would be the man to seek out as to why the plan was not working.

Sickles contacted Lincoln and Stanton to request further military assignments. There must be something he could do even with his diminished capacity. When in Washington, he was welcomed at the White House and to Edwin Stanton's home on K Street.

Dan was now forty-four, but looked years younger, slim, handsome, and always immaculately dressed, as he had always been all of his life. He returned to New York City and took rooms at the Brevort House, a fine hotel on lower Fifth Avenue. Teresa and Laura were still living in Bloomingdale, and it is not known if there was any contact now between the three of them. Dan felt that it was important for him to be nearer the city, where his many friends and political allies lived and worked.

He wrote Lincoln again, stating his availability as a person who would be in charge of a military commission to go between Washington and the Southern states to become better acquainted with the Southern people, and their politicians and clergymen. Lincoln telegraphed back very soon to offer him a trip to Arkansas,[1] and Sickles accepted, although it was not exactly what he had in mind, but it was a start and he jumped at the opportunity to help the Union in almost any capacity. President Lincoln had told Sickles that he had "plans" for him immediately after his wounding on the day he had arrived in Washington from Gettysburg, and this could lead to more important posts in the future.

Before leaving for the trip South, Sickles was invited to the White House for a reception for General Grant, after his being made the first Lieutenant General since George Washington. Grant was ill at ease with such a fancy reception, but held out his hand to thousands of well wishers, including Dan. They were introduced by Secretary of War Stanton. The next day Sickles and Grant met at Willard's over some Kentucky bourbon and started a friendship that would last all of their remaining years. They both liked Lincoln and they talked of that, and although the two of them were different from each other, they shared a bond of fighting spirit. Sickles asked Grant to help put down a plan he had learned about, to consolidate the remaining Third Corps into the Second Corps when the Army of the Potomac was being reorganized. Grant explained that he had delegated as much executive power as he could to General Meade in regard to matters of administration, and that he could not meddle in this now after so soon taking over as commander.

The trip to Arkansas, planned for February 15, 1864, turned out to be a longer one than was first spoken of to Sickles. It was now to be a tour of investigation, stopping at such places as Memphis, Helena, Vicksburg, New Orleans, Pensacola, Key West, and Charleston Harbor, to determine what was being done, if anything, for Reconstruction and amnesty programs.

Information was to be gathered on the colored people and how they were getting along as hired laborers, both in and out of Rebel lines. Whether there were deserters in from the Confederate Armies, and if enough of them had knowledge of the amnesty.[2]

Dan left with Major Tremain and a staff of five headed South. The Military Governor of Tennessee was Andrew Johnson, who was a hard liner about the evils of slavery and there were complaints about his harshness to all citizens of the state. Dan met with the governor for the first time and would certainly meet him again in the future as Lincoln's vice-president.

While on this tour, Dan had occasion to visit the field camp of Generals Hooker and Butterfield, the two under General Sherman's command, and there again was "back in the field with his old and good friends, for a short time, living like a soldier."[3] This must have been a fine time for Dan and his comrades. He stayed to witness the Battle of Resaca, Georgia. There must have been much talk about George Meade, as all three of them disliked him intensely, and he must have been the subject of a lot of talk in the tent with the three generals there together for the first time in more than a year.

Sickles stopped at Helena, Arkansas, and found much hatred and hostile attitude towards reconstruction and the North in general. After touring all of the stops to determine the state of the reconstruction plans, Dan concluded his trip with a visit to Charleston Harbor, where the war had started.

Dan had been gone from April till August, when he returned to Washington to give the president a lengthy report in person, then on to New York City to await further orders to report for any future actions necessary, for which he might be called.

Another presidential election campaign was starting up, and Lincoln had been nominated along with Andrew Johnson, whom Sickles had met in Tennessee. The Democrats had selected and nominated General George McClellan for president and George Pendleton for vice-president. The same Pendleton who was the brother-in-law of Philip Barton Key, whom Dan had shot and killed. Their platform was to be a "quick end to the war."

Dan learned of the death from malaria of General David Birney and was sad to hear of his sudden death, even though he had contracted the disease during the Seven Days before Richmond Battles, quite awhile ago.

Sickles hatched a new plan to Lincoln to have the Third Corps reorganized with himself at its head. He felt that good officers, such as Hooker, Butterfield, and himself had been passed over and had had their day of glory, which was no more. New names were in the papers now, and the dream of these three men to return to better command to help end the war was only a dream, and the generals being used were doing pretty well without them.

The election was overwhelmingly in favor of Lincoln, and his vice-president, Andrew Johnson. The war was progressing to a possible ending, with the South being squeezed by both generals, Grant and Sherman. Dan waited and waited, but no orders were forthcoming, and again he wrote to Lincoln with a plea to be reassigned. Healthy, competent, and fit for duty, the letter that he wrote was one of dismay at not being called upon, as were many officers, and their being dropped from the rolls of the army. He literally begged for reconsideration and Lincoln could not refuse with his letter signed, "From your friend and servant," and called Dan to come to Washington.

Arriving in Washington, Sickles learned that he was not to be given responsibilities in the army, but was being called for a special, confidential mission to go to Panama and Colombia to seek permission of the government there for colonization of freed American slaves. This offer, though not what he wanted, was important and filled with action and prestige. That was enough for him right now.

In January 1865, he sailed from New York City. Standing and waving from the dock were Teresa, now twenty-nine years old, Laura, and their good friend, Wikoff. Teresa was crying, although it was not her way to do anything but conceal her feelings lately, and Wikoff said that Laura, now an impressionable twelve-year-old, was also crying, the first time he had ever seen her do so. These words were written to Dan by him, so Dan realized what this departure meant to his family, and he probably did have some contact with them, if only to say good-bye. He was pleased to be making the trip and they knew what the president's offer of assistance meant to him. They both must have been filled with pride, the two of them, wife still, mother and daughter, loving this man who was so close and yet so far removed from their lives for four years and more that he was involved in the army and the war.

George Sickles was very curious about his son's trip and the purpose behind it, but knew none of the details, of course. He wrote to Dan of Laura's visit to her grandmother as a general thing on Saturdays, and sometimes stops overnight, assumed to have been with her paternal grandparents, George Sickles and his wife, Susan. Both parents of Teresa and Daniel Sickles were alive at this time, although quite elderly, but giving all the support possible to their only grandchild, Laura Buchanan Sickles.

The trip started in Panama, where Dan heard talk of a possible canal being built to bring access between two oceans that would affect shipping the world over. The journey from there to Bogota, Colombia, included a long river passage done only in the rainy season.

Sickles's meetings were with President Murillo, who had been Colombia's minister in Washington when Dan was a Congressman, and he was well known to him. This was an important fact of friendship, which kept returning in Dan's life again and again.

This trip took from January to early June on 1865. Sickles had hoped to return before the ending of the war, and wrote to Stanton of his hope in a letter, reporting his progress in negotiations for Negro colonization and receiving permission for the passage of troops across Panama. By July 1st, he anticipated being back in Washington to remind Stanton again of his desire to be put in a program for reconstruction in South Carolina, as in the interim, Charleston, Colombia, and Wilmington had fallen. He stressed that he would be reporting to him, "standing on two legs," having made use of his artificial leg, riding over difficult mountain roads and that even General Meade would not doubt his ability to ride far enough to the front tollpost a battery" or make a reconnaissance.

On April 6th, General Lee surrendered to General Grant at Appomattox Courthouse and the tide of war had flowed out. Sickles hurried home as fast as possible, making the wearisome trip, hoping to insure himself that no one else would be considered for the post he desired the most. Along the trip home, he was handed a dispatch that shook him terribly. President Lincoln had been shot and died soon after, and that mistakenly both Stanton and Seward had received mortal wounds. He anguished many days about this development until receiving the truth that only President Lincoln was dead. It had been hard to believe that all three of such good friends had succumbed to assassination bullets. Washington must be in total chaos!

After the grueling trip that could not be hurried, he landed in New York City to deliver many crates of wild animals to the Central Park Zoo, which he brought along to present to the park, of which he was so proud.

Enough time had passed, by then, since the assassination that John Wilkes Booth had been killed, his accomplices captured and tried. Jefferson Davis was a prisoner, and now the country must heal and put itself back to becoming one nation. This would be a formidable undertaking.

Dan knew that Andrew Johnson, now the president, had been a staunch hater of Southern ways and would try to deal harshly with the vanquished citizens of the South. However, Dan had come to know him well from his trip to Nashville when they shared a mint julep together and they had become allies in spirit. Now Dan had known the last four presidents and had been on good terms with them. He knew that he was the man for the job of bringing orders to South Carolina, as he had the political and diplomatic experience that this job would entail.

The beautiful cities of Charleston and Columbia were

in utter ruin by the progression of General Sherman's men, businesses closed, and Negroes and idle ex-Confederate soldiers milling around with nothing to do. There was famine, suffering, and seething hate, which remained in many hearts and minds.

Into this frenzied territory came Dan Sickles, who somehow had to turn chaos into stability. The ones who were being hurt the most were Negroes and poor whites, including what was left of the remaining veterans. The plantation owners now had no help unless they hired laborers, and there was little money for that. A committee of important citizens of Charleston came to Dan, whose headquarters was now in a fine house, to offer their services as they were able. The most immediate goal was to provide food, which was in very scant supply, and assurance that he wanted to help them with all the problems that affected them. The citizens would have to work, even freed Negroes would be required to toil. Sickles found that his old friend, James L. Orr, another Washington congressman and former occupant of the Stockton Mansion in Washington, was the Provisional Governor of South Carolina. Here was another old friend from the past returning. It was almost uncanny how often this turned out to have become a routine occurrence. Sickles now had seven thousand soldiers working for him and Governor Orr, and the two men overcame the obstacles with food, jobs, and a sincere dedication to unify South Carolina again.

By the next winter, some degree of order was seen, and men were elected to civil office again to begin the process. General Grant stopped in Charleston on a tour of the South, and was pleased at what he saw, as a new start to solving the many complex problems. Sickles gave him a grand dinner at his headquarters to which Governor Orr was invited along with other Southerners. The Reconstruction plans started off well, with citizens waiting to see how any new orders would be accepted and effect them. Congress, however, was filled with determined members, who as Dixie-hating radicals were gaining control. They maintained that the freed Southern Negroes must be granted equality with whites, including the right to vote. To white Southerners, this was unthinkable, seeing that the ratio of black to white was overwhelmingly in favor of blacks, possibly running for office, becoming legislators, and even governor!

Daniel Sickles could see that this would be an impossible assignment, treading the thin line between pacifying blacks and whites. He wrote Stanton that in most cases the ex-slaves could not read or write and their signatures were an X. They had not been trained to be citizens, and that would take a lot of time to accomplish. Meanwhile, the Southern whites were seething and some silently threatened the Negroes to "keep low," and there were random acts of violence committed.

The whites met in secret to counteract the Negro menace that they foresaw arriving. Dan's troubles were doubled in June of 1866, as he was appointed to the Department of the Carolina, adding North Carolina to increase the responsibilities of having to maintain the more than two million people this department encompassed. There was also violence against the Federal soldiers, who were there to maintain order. This was when nightly riders with hoods came on the land to threaten the blacks further.

The populace realized that it was not Sickles and the Union soldiers who threatened them, but the Congress in Washington, who were still punishing the South for starting the war to begin with. The Dixie-hating radicals were in the forefront and "pushing down" with all of their weight. Sickles could not tolerate this breech of the peace. He was there to enforce and he instituted martial law. He used arrests and even cavalrymen to enforce the policies of no firearms, even by the local departments.

These harsh measures being taken were heard of by President Andrew Johnson, who although he felt pity for the Southerners, as did Lincoln before him, did not know how to deal with the radicals in Congress, and so pounced on Sickles, knowing his penchant for controversy. Sickles viewed these as necessary acts, but Johnson viewed them as too harsh and perhaps a more temperate solution would suffice. However, he knew that Dan had powerful friends in Grant and Stanton, who would back him, and Johnson realized this and could not allow any loss of political allies. As a follower of Lincoln, among the top elected officials of the land, he had to tread a thin line to survive. Move the general out!

His plan was to offer Sickles a foreign plum, the position of Minister of the Netherlands, a post that Dan turned down as being too expensive a location, seeing that his family would live "only" in New York, and he would have to have two homes, one being large enough for doing diplomatic work. He would accept a post in either St. Petersburg, Berlin, Paris, Florence, or Madrid. Dan stayed in Charleston, and Teresa and Laura stayed in New York City. It had been seven years of this arrangement. He could have had his family with him now, of course, but he knew that Teresa would be a social pariah as a diplomat's wife, a result of her mad affair, and his shooting of Key, so long ago. Laura, at this time, was a growing girl unknown to him. Too much time had elapsed. It was best that mother and the ever-growing child should stay where both families could watch over them. It had been too long for Dan to take charge of them.

Dan, now forty-seven, one legged, and handsome still, was not long consoling himself with a charmer named Allie

Grant, whose letter to him in June, not fully understood, was kept as part of his personal papers now in the New York Public Library, in New York City. Surely, he would not have kept such a letter unless it and she meant something in his life. We shall never know. . . .

In February, Dan Sickles made a sad trip to New York City. His wife, Teresa, had died after failing health. It is said that she had a cold, which could quite possibly have turned into pneumonia, but on her death certificate of February 5, 1867, the cause of death is listed as anaemia, or hemorrhage, and her age at thirty.[4] She had been taking sedatives for some time to help with sleep. This may have contributed to her death, but I believe that she died from a lack of control over her life, having lost that on February 27nd, 1859. She probably had a case of severe depression and an unfixable broken heart. She lived only for her daughter, but could not continue as she was with her health problems.

Her funeral was held at Saint Joseph's Roman Catholic Church in New Rochelle. Four generals were among the pallbearers: Major General Alfred Pleasonton, Third Corps cavalry commander; Major General Gordon Granger, hero of Chickamauga and Chattanooga; Brigadier General Charles K. Graham, one of Dan's best friends and one of his brigade commanders; and Brigadier General Henry Tremain, war-time aide-de-camp, who had stood beside Dan for years before and after his wounding at Gettysburg. Also in attendance were James Brady, John Krug, Otto Gabriotti, William Field, and Edward Vermylie.

Dan, Laura, Signor and Signora Bagioli, Henry Wikoff, and George G. Sickles, the general's father were seated near the altar for the simple and moving ceremony to honor the young woman. Dan may not have had the courage to admit that he shared the blame for her depth of despair and it is said that he was deeply in grief, remembering the dark-eyed and black-haired young child who grew into his love, until the unthinkable happened.

Laura was thirteen and a tragic figure at the funeral, with her head bowed and huddled in a corner of a pew, vaguely aware of the meaning of the feelings of anger and shame stirred by her father, almost a stranger now.

The worst possible age for a young girl to lose her mother, after having "lost" her father years ago. Teresa's coffin of fine rosewood with a silver plaque giving her name, age, and date of death, covered with lovely fragrant flowers of which she was so fond, was placed in front of the high altar of the church surrounded by burning tapers.

Teresa was eulogized by the Rev. Thomas Farrell with words of touching tenderness to the deceased and with warm condolences to her parents and bereaved husband. Words were spoken of the loyalty of her husband to his country and the cause of union and freedom for which he had paid through hardships and loss, now of his wife, the treasure of his life. He must look to God to sustain him in this hour. The family left the church, filled with friends and strangers who once outside gave vent to their emotions with love and good will from their hearts.

Teresa was buried temporarily in a Catholic cemetery on Second Avenue, in New York City, where Lorenzo Da Ponte had been placed in an unmarked grave. She was later reburied in Greenwood Cemetery in Brooklyn, New York. In the family plot are now resting together, the following family members of the immediate family. Teresa Bagioli Sickles, Antonio Bagioli, Teresa's father; Eliza Bagioli, Teresa's mother; Susan March Sickles, the first wife of George Garrett Sickles, and mother of Daniel Edgar Sickles; and Laura Buchanan Sickles Carlton, the daughter of Teresa and Daniel Sickles. Susan Sickles died in Paris in 1879, where she had been living with her son, Daniel, for many years. She was returned from France and was buried in Greenwood Cemetery at a later date.

Dan returned to Charleston with Laura, hoping somehow to become the "father to the child." It was to be a difficult transition, which I imagine both families understood. There was some initial resistance to her attending a fashionable academy of Madame Tivane, who objected to enrolling the daughter of such a heritage in her school. The headmistress of another academy, Mrs. Alston, gladly accepted Laura as a student, adding that if any parent objected, a place should be found in another academy for their daughter.[5]

Slowly, Laura regained some of her composure among her companions and location, but she was moody and confused by this sudden change in her different living arrangements. Her heritage came from a beautiful mother, and her father's temperament of headstrong will. Dan was not used to dealing with an adolescent and the time it would take away from his busy schedule to work at it seriously enough to help them both adjust to one another.

Dan wrote to President Johnson to request a post in the permanent military organization, corresponding to the grade that he had reached as a volunteer officer in the field during the war. This letter was written on black-edged stationary, noting bereavement of a personal loss, that of his wife. Nothing came of this letter.

Running concurrent with his personal problems were even more serious ones for the Carolinas. Bankruptcy was rampant in both states and the backlog of suits to collect owing funds was more than 60,000. There were penniless widows of veterans and even homeless veterans themselves were being put in prison for debt. Governor Orr called on Dan for help to forbid this practice. Dan issued another order, this one number ten on a growing list, to protect the citizens from jail and small properties from foreclosure. Naturally some supported the move, and some thought Sickles too high-handed and should be removed.

Politics being what it is, the wind of peace was shifting and Sickles was in the middle. He truly did help the average citizen of both states, but some of his policies were not in line with state politicians and federal judges. Both Dan and Stanton were now running contrary to the Johnson team. Stanton was dismissed, and Sickles, angry about this, asked to be relieved of command, saying, "The declaration of the Attorney General, disarms me of means to protect life, property, or the rights of citizens and menaces all interests in these states with ruin."

Upon receipt of this letter, President Johnson was furious and on August 27th 1867, he relieved Sickles of his office. For almost two years, Sickles had been trying to bring calm and order out of chaos, but the time was over for this, through his part in it, so he returned to New York, vowing to work to remove President Johnson from office!

Congress had passed EVERY bill that Johnson had vetoed! Dan's friend, Stanton, was out, and Grant was appointed the interim of Secretary of War. Sickles and Philip Sheridan, the latter also a military commander-in-chief in Texas, Louisiana, and Tennessee, were feted at a reception given by Grant, which showed where he stood! Stanton's removal was judged to be illegal and he was reinstated. This seesaw of command was coming at a furious pace. There was even talk of impeachment, and a committee was formed to prepare the articles if it came to that.

Ulysses Grant, a popular figure since the ending of the war, was looked on as a candidate who would be firm, tactful, and a man of good sense. These were Sickles's words and he could visualize Grant as president, once

Johnson was dispensed with. This possible realization began with the impeachment trial of President Johnson, which began in March of 1868, with the Senate as judges, and with Chief Justice Chase presiding. If the trial were to finish Johnson, then Chase would succeed the President as Chief Justice, as the law was set up during that time.

Dan Sickles had decided to be the first to back Grant, and in doing so left the Democratic Party, to which he had been allied for thirty years. He had backed Lincoln, who was a Republican, with his vote and confidence, but he still considered himself a Democrat from the start in the Tammany organization when he first entered politics in New York City.

Now he found himself chosen for chairman of the New York delegation to the Republican National Convention in Chicago, Illinois. Dan was sure that if Grant were elected, he would not be forgotten and would find new outlets for his many labors in the political arena. While waiting for developments, he busied himself with his law practice to which he could always return and make substantial money, which he had started to invest in stocks, as most men were doing at that time. After the war, the country started manufacturing and supplying consumer goods that had to be replaced after the long war. The country was booming!

In March of 1869, Grant was inaugurated as president and a grand ball was held at the Treasury Building.[6] Dan was there on crutches, not dancing, but "working the crowd." Finally, Grant offered him the office of Minister to Spain. Grant's Secretary of War, John Rawlins, was eager to acquire Cuba and knew that Sickles had always considered this move just what he wanted done if possible.

Before Dan set sail for Spain, Grant awarded him the honor of being made a full Major General in the regular army, one of the highest honors paid to any soldier after the close of the Civil War. The one "fly in the ointment" was a Johnson administration act that forbid any army officer to take nonmilitary positions in foreign missions, and if they were to do so, would forfeit their commissions. Dan wanted the Ministership, but NOT under the rules of the act, and give up his generalship, so he went directly to Grant with the question. The president told him that since he was now a retired general and the mission to Spain did not require army pay, he would NOT lose his commission. There was a good reception given by Dan's many friends on June 30th, 1869 to toast his appointment. The location was Everett House, where a celebration had been held thirteen years before when James Buchanan returned from England.

Two hundred guests toasted Dan that night.

Blistering attacks were published in New York City newspapers, calling Sickles every villainous name. They brought up every scandalous and immoral story available, including Fanny White, his murderous act of shooting Key. Nothing was left out in print for the readers to be thoroughly informed about the latest new diplomat.

Sickles was off on another new adventure, sailing to Spain, taking his mother, Susan, and leaving his father at home in New Rochelle.

Laura was along under the care of her loving grandmother, who would be hostess for her son, Daniel Sickles, at the legation in Madrid. The start of a new life? That remained to be seen. . . . .

Twelve
Isabella and Paris

Dan arrived in Madrid in July 1869 and took a large suite in the Hotel De Russia for himself and his mother and Laura. His mother had had a domestic quarrel with Dan's father and had accompanied her son to Spain, and never returned home before her death in 1874, in a sanatorium in Paris. She was a charming lady whom Dan treated with the utmost respect and love, and she was able, even at an advanced age, to function beautifully at this essential task of being the official hostess for the American Legation for her son. George Sickles, like his son, Dan, was not one to live without the company of women for too long. Dan did not know that his length of stay in Europe would be eight years and a second life would commence.

Sickles's personal goal was "to trade cash for Cuba," which he had long sought years ago. The Queen of Spain, Maria Christina, who was regent for her infant daughter, Isabella, sought to trade Cuba and the Philippines to France for a small sum of money, this plan failing.

Two times the United States government had upped the price considerably, only to be turned down. At this time, Spain was in bankruptcy and on the brink of civil war, and another quiet try might result in success. Persistent diplomacy would need to be used for the country to turn over a colony far away, drawing on Spain's short supply of cash unmercifully.

There were five political parties plotting to take over the land, and upon Maria Christina's exile to France, with Isabella, and a vast retinue, General Prim was made commander-in-chief of the Spanish Army, and Marshall Serrano, the interim premier, were in charge now. Adding to the warring factions, was the pretender, Don Carlos. Sickles believed that Spain needed a new monarch, a tradition of one thousand years, to be put back on the throne. The Queen Mother and Isabella were exiled and living in France, and spending Spain into poverty quickly. Surely trading Cuba for cash would appeal to the Spanish Exchequer, thought Sickles. Raising the Stars and Stripes over Cuba would alarm both England and France, which had to be considered seriously.

Dan was allowed to bring up the proposal with the utmost secrecy to General Prim only and start off in a suggestive narration to feel out the general! Sickles, as usual, worked his magnetic charm. Late in 1869, Prim and Serrano agreed to a constitutional monarchy as their choice of a new Spanish government. There were three claimants to the throne: Don Carlos, the pretender; Isabella's eleven-year-old son, Alfonso; and Isabella's brother-in-law, the Duc de Montpensier.

Sickles maintained that Spain could stabilize her finances, and pave the way for a smooth transition to a monarchy, if his plan, so carefully mentioned to General Prim were considered. Prim said he would decide if there were no words about Sickles's plan to escape to the press or public. Meanwhile, a search for a new king was started. One by one the candidates were found and eliminated, and at length, Prim himself was eliminated by an assassin's bullet, by an unknown assailant. Gone was Sickles's hope for a smooth transition.

Laura was now sixteen, a thin, wild, and strangely beautiful young woman who almost at once, fell madly in love with a young Spanish officer. Her father would have none of that, and she had a reckless affair. He intervened, and the carefully tended affection that he had hoped would appear in new surroundings with a new relationship between them that would finally be a true father-daughter one. This was not to be, as Laura would take no controlling and would show nothing but defiant conduct to her father.

Sickles moved in court circles, although there was no court, in reality, but there were members of the Bourbon bloodlines who managed to hang on with some degree to the noble life in Spain, while their exiled possible rulers lived in France awaiting the decisions ahead.

He met the widowed marquise, a devoted friend of Isabella all of her life. The marquise's young daughter, Carolina or Caroline, was acting as lady-in-waiting to the exiled queen. The Creaghs were of noble Irish stock and connected to the Royal Bodyguards of Carlos III.

Dan became intrigued with these new friendships and when diplomatic affairs brought him to Paris, the marquise asked him to please stop in Biarritz and deliver some confidential papers to Isabella. He remembered meeting her many years ago and enjoyed thinking about the beguiling creature who had set her expression on him with the intent of perhaps making a more than fleeting impression. He was eager to see for himself how she greeted him now, on crutches, one leg, older, but still handsome at forty-nine, not looking that age at all.

Isabella was using the Chateau Mont Orr for her time in exile. Sickles was received alone by the queen. He knew of her long, sometimes bizarre pleasure-loving and high-spending past, and she undoubtedly knew the same about his past life, and so they had many similar lifestyles.

Isabella, still beautiful, sparkling black eyes and long black hair, an overly plump seductress, who had had many a lover, was about to work her magic on another, who was up to her wiles and knew methods of his own through much experience with the feminine gender. She was curious to inquire if he believed that her young son, now eleven years old, Alfonso, could become king. Dan agreed that he thought this would no doubt happen, "in the future," as Alfonso was the most practical solution of a monarch for Spain.

Prince Amedeo of Savoy, son of the king of Italy, had agreed to become king of Spain, although he was viewed as a foreigner who should not govern the country. Sickles brought up his plan for Cuba to Amedeo, but it was not seriously considered or discussed, with all of the seething discontent and violence. War waged in Cuba and Dan's mission was striking barriers and all he could do was ask and wait, and ask and wait some more.

Sickles was an excellent host and the entertainment he offered his guests outgrew the suite at the Hotel de Russia, so he rented a finely furnished house for his family at Number 12 Calle Isabella Catolica. Here he met with the cream of Spanish society, and was able to discuss with equal competence the works of artists, food and wines, opera, and Gettysburg, of which he had first-hand knowledge. Nor were women left out of his life, as they were as much a passion as the political life he lived.

At one of these salons happened to be the daughter of the Marquise Creagh, Carolina, whose father had died when she was an infant, and had taken the name of her stepfather, Senor Jose Greagh. She had been in a convent school, as had been Teresa Sickles, and now was a twenty-some-year-old lovely Spanish senorita. She had also taken a helpful interest in Laura Sickles, and Dan had taken an

Queen Isabella II of Spain was General Sickles's most famous mistress.

interest in her! Laura was doing somewhat better now, as she had found friends her own age, and was studying the German language, as Dan wrote to his friend Charles Graham and his wife, Mary. He added that in his home was a room for them whenever they could come for a visit in Spain.[1] Dan's mother, Susan, was still the official hostess and doing well so far, as to her health.

John Milton Hay, who had been the younger of President Lincoln's two secretaries in Washington, was now the secretary of the American Legation under Sickles. The two had known each other years ago. Hay wrote to Robert Lincoln, the president's eldest son, that he did not like Madrid a lot, but that the ladies were beautiful, including Laura Sickles and her friends, who seemed to be enjoying themselves.[2]

John Hay was offered an editorial post on *The New York Tribune,* under Horace Greeley, and left for home. As a new secretary, Dan was able to get his friend Charles Graham's nephew, Alvey Augustus Adee, to come to Spain to take the vacant position.

Isabella had lived a rather sordid and dissolute life, forced at sixteen to marry a cousin, and rebelled with numerous affairs. She had five children, most of whose fathers were whispered about. She was now forty-one, a true Bohemian, as any free-thinking and acting person was referred to in that era. She was warm-hearted and easy-going and enjoyed spending money and living life to its fullest. A true "simpatico" to what she had heard of Dan Sickles.

The general and Isabella started a romance together and soon were seen in each other's company whenever the two met in Paris, where she had a sumptuous home on the Avenue Kleber. The affair became general knowledge and Paris buzzed with talk about the Queen and "Le Roi Americain de L'Espagne," The Yankee King of Spain!

The two of them so alike, not caring about convention, going to the opera, shopping madly on the boulevards, and being seen and noticed as Dan, maneuvering on his crutches, and laughing as they moved along, stopping for tea and pastries at Angelina's on La Rue Di Rivoli. They understood each other, and thoroughly enjoyed each other's company. Dan had finally met a woman who had lived as hard as he had, and could still laugh heartily at life. Behind all of this merriment, Isabella knew that it was a happy interval, and that she was the daughter of King Ferdinand VII, and God willing would hold the throne again. She wanted the Bourbon line restored through her son, Alfonso, and she would wait and hope this would happen. Her supporters were outraged by this open affair with the one-legged general, and worse, the American Minister, as they felt that the affair would imperil the naming of her son back to the throne of Spain.

Sickles had decided in despair that his plan for Cuba had been shelved by the reign of King Amadeo, the ruler himself having been shot at on several occasions. The only course left was to seek his abdication. Although it was forbidden by the State Department for a minister of a country to meddle in its internal affairs, this was just what Dan was doing after his decision to support a group advocating revolution, and establishing a republic with the possible return of the monarchy and Prince Alfonso. Two years had gone by and Dan was no further ahead. His lifetime creed of "decision followed by action," was about to be put to use again.

By the autumn of 1871, Sickles had wooed and won Carolina Creagh. It was thought that perhaps he indeed loved her, as she loved him, and this union might bring fulfillment and possibly children to them. It must have offered something very personal to Dan to remarry at the

Carolina Creagh, known as Caroline Amador Guerrero Sickles at the time of her marriage to Daniel E. Sickles.

age of fifty-two after so many nonformalized relationships before. He converted to Roman Catholicism, and the banns were published, with the couple to be wed in the spring. Dan had been involved with the Jay Gould affair back in the United States, and had another concurrent plan to force Gould from control of the Erie Railroad.

To convict Gould of corruption and theft was against the better judgment of the company and the stockholders. Inasmuch as Dan would have to return to New York City in secret about this course, he decided to marry sooner and take his bride back with him on a honeymoon.

The ceremony took place at the American Legation in Madrid on November 28th, 1871, with General Serrano and many foreign ministers were in attendance.[3] Dan's mother and Caroline's parents were there, along with Laura, who was a bridesmaid. The bride looked lovely and happy even though her husband was more than twice her age and would never be able to change his ways. It has been written that this marriage might have been a ploy to take attention from the affair of Queen Isabella and Sickles, but I believe that there must have been more to this marriage than that idea, than to have Caroline act as a "sacrificial lamb being offered for slaughter," the lamb being Caroline. The bride was listed on the marriage certificate as Carolina Martinez Amador Guerrero with the signature of A. Augustus Adee of the American Legation.

Isabella knew that the end must come at some time to the affair with Sickles, and probably did not object to his loss to her and marriage to Caroline, knowing full well her desire to have her son, Alfonso, returned to the throne. She, like Sickles, was seldom unaware of the goals set and the way to success and accepted the change. Both Dan's love, and her son, the king, back on the throne were not possible.

They were realists and knew that they must move on with their lives. If, however, they were to meet again?

President Grant had given Dan a leave of absence for three months so he could oust Jay Gould from control, whom he maintained had robbed the Erie Railroad of sixty million dollars, with help from "Boss" William Marcy Tweed, who was a member of Erie's Board of Directors. The two of them master-minding the cannibalization of the Erie Railroad. Dan and Caroline landed in New York on December 22nd, 1871, on a combination honeymoon and the battle for the Erie Railroad. The latter took over with the most importance, and Caroline must have spent much of her time alone in a new and strange land for her. Not a good way to start a new life with a new husband and a different country. Dan visited President Grant in Washington, then returned to New York City to start the battle. Interestingly enough, General McClellan, as president of the Atlantic and Great Western Railroad, was aligned with the group to unseat Gould. After a loud session, at the end of Dan's three-month leave of absence, Gould resigned and Dan received as much press coverage as with Gettysburg. As a result of this success, Dan was given a large block of Erie Stock and ownership of his rented house at 23 Fifth Avenue, where he was to spend the rest of his life in New York City.

Sickles and Caroline sailed back to Spain on April 27th, not knowing what he would find in his absence from the Legation. The war in Cuba was more than three years old and relations had worsened. Upon his return, Dan dove back into the scheme of insurrection against King Amedeo.

Caroline presented Dan with a daughter, whom they named Edith and called Eda, and a year later, a son was born, also in Madrid, whom they called George Stanton Sickles, named for Dan's father and Edwin Stanton, the former Secretary of War, Dan's friend, and his chief defense lawyer during the trial for killing Philip Barton Key.

Laura was refusing to accept Caroline and would no longer live with them, so she left for New York City. Never really happy for so long a time, she reportedly married a butcher, named Carlton, a last name only known, and soon left him to live on a small allowance provided by her father. She is said to have taken to drinking. A sad end for the once happy little girl, who adored her parents, and whose life had gone steadily downhill since that fateful day in 1859, to die at age thirty-eight. Nothing can be found out about the funeral service, or if any family members were present. It might be assumed that some were, although her father, Daniel, was not in attendance. She was buried in the unnamed plot at Greenwood Cemetery with other immediate family members. George Garrett Sickles owned both family plots, Greenwood and Beechwood, in Brooklyn and New Rochelle, respectively.

There was more trouble with the Virginians episode. The ship, flying an American flag, a blockade runner, had been bringing arms into Cuba to aid the insurrectionists. It was captured by a Spanish ship and there was murder in the death of its American captain and fifty-two crewmen. The United States was greatly angered and talk of war was heard. Sickles, who had been honored before, was now the villain, and with war possibly coming, he handed in his resignation. He had gone too far by making policy, instead of obeying the policies of the United States.

Secretary of State Hamilton Fish was faced with a serious crisis. The country was clamoring for war to avenge the murders, and Fish was trying to avert such confrontation. Dan was instructed to remain at his post. A negotiated settlement was devised, and Dan Sickles was forced to resign amid the comment, "good riddance." Gone was Dan's long thought of someday becoming president, which had lain dormant, except in the furthest recesses of his mind.

In February, Sickles left Spain for Paris, with his wife and children, and his mother, Susan. The new minister to the American Legation would be arriving in the person of Caleb Cushing. For the first time, Dan would not be involved in maneuvering. He loved Paris, spoke fluent French, and Caroline did not want to move to an unknown land, the United States.

Isabella had bought the Hotel Basilewski, renamed it the Palace of Castile, and was continuing to live lavishly on an allowance, awaiting the return of her son to the throne. Dan's mother, in advancing years, was placed in a Paris sanitorium. She died and was buried in France until being returned to America to lie finally in Greenwood Cemetery in New York, in the vault with other family members.

There was a rumor again of General Sickles seeing Isabella, which Caroline must have heard about, learning of his definition of marriage, which was quite different from hers. Dan installed Caroline and the two children on an estate near Chantilly, and he took rooms in the center of Paris, to be near Isabella. The very warm feeling that they had for each other returned, as might be expected. It is hard to fathom why this might be true with a wife and two small children, but Dan was Dan, and he might have felt more comfortable with a woman who understood him so well. Perhaps he wanted it both ways, another, a father of two offspring to extend the Sickles's line down through the ages, or perhaps the children were Caroline's deep wish only.

About this time, Dan was awarded the medal of a Commander of the Legion of Honor from France for his services to the French government, an honor that he cherished.

Sickles made many trips to the United States, especially to Washington, where he would spend six months or more, mending fences and renewing friendships for the time spent in Europe. He went again in early 1878, to Newburgh, New York, to a reunion of the Third Corps Union. There the grizzled old veterans of Chancellorsville and Gettysburg, Hooker, Twichell, and others he knew well, again the camaraderie of the good old days. He told them that he expected to return for good in the autumn. Dan knew that his European ventures were nearly over.

Early in 1875, Isabella's son was crowned King Alfonso XII, and she was returned, not with any affection to her subjects, but as Queen Mother, who would stand with him.[4] Her dream was realized. . . . .

Sickles, expecting this at last, could see his life slipping relentlessly away. Where had the years gone? For eight years he had been caught in the backwater of political life in Europe, really going nowhere, and the way to get back on track, especially with the election of 1880 ahead, was overpowering.

He went to Chantilly to see Caroline with the news that they were all leaving for America and to pack up! Caroline, whose mother was ill in Madrid, wanted to go back there, and refused to go to America.

She had also found out about Isabella's affair with her husband and "that he had been untrue to me." Dan wanted no more of Madrid, a place that was in the past and so in truth gone from the future. There surely must have been tears and hysterics from the lady, and even Dan, who loved his children, I am sure, put ambition for the remainder of his life ahead of his family life, although for most men, that decision would have been to hard to bear. A sad parting for all concerned, but once a decision is made, there is no turning back. Dan was staking everything on one more political attempt at a comeback.

Caroline took their daughter, Eda, and their son, Stanton, with her returning to her mother's home in Madrid. And so began a long separation. . . . .

Thirteen

Home Again and Back to Congress: First Priority, Gettysburg

Dan, now sixty-one, opened his home at twenty-three Fifth Avenue, New York City. He still did not look his age, and although the public thought of him as being only fifty-seven, as he had taken to stating that he was born in 1825, he believed still that was a white lie for a politician who still had ambition. Since his leaving eight years before, there were now telephones, electric lights in some places, elevated railroads, and a bridge in Brooklyn. Unfortunately, many of Sickles's friends were gone. Hooker, Sherman, and Mrs. Bagioli were still living, but her husband, Antonio had died. Dan Butterfield also lived on in the city.

One of Dan's neighbors was seen stopping in, Mark Twain, and they shared many good times.[1] Dan filled the house with all sorts of flags and banners, stuffed animals from all over the world, crossed swords, medals, a veritable museum of war regalia, plus many photographs of friends in high and low places, and other warriors. Dan liked to surround himself with the accouterments of his military service.

When Sickles returned, he again took up service as a lawyer. He was appalled by the distress that he saw on the streets, of veterans begging from passersby to sustain what was left of their crippled years ahead. He was genuinely moved by their plight and took charge of a campaign to establish a state soldier's home. He became increasingly aware of these men, who unlike himself, had no recourse but to beg help from their fellow countrymen. He now had a new goal in his life and threw himself in every possible way to help the forgotten wounded. He lobbied for pension allowances, even to opening his own home to any veteran who needed his help, to using his own money, whenever the doorbell rang, and a veteran was found on the stoop.

Also in residence at 23 Fifth Avenue, was an unmarried, rather plain young middle-aged woman, named Eleanora Earle Wilmerding. She was the Sickles's housekeeper and secretary, along with an aging Negro, Frazier Mosley, who had been Dan's valet and good friend for many years, moving from house to house in the United States, from Bloomingdale to Washington, and to 23 Fifth Avenue, New York City.

Eleanora came from a well-bred and well-thought-of family. Her position in the household was questioned as to just what her duties there. She referred to Dan, as "Dear," but that in itself would not be too familiar under most instances. She has been called his last mistress, although perhaps only a good friend for thirty years. I guess the answer will remain hidden. She was a quiet lady and committed to tending her charge in later years with much devotion and affection.

If she was in the household for thirty years, she would have been quite young at first. Dan would have been only sixty-four years old, and there might have been a relationship. She was well aware of his many lady friends, but kept quiet, happy just to be with their friend, who could still exercise great charm and charisma over the ladies.

There was always physical intimacy between Dan and the women in his life, but no holding tightly. He had to have free rein regardless.

The 1886 reunion of the Battle of Gettysburg. From left to right are: Brigadier General Joseph B. Carr, Major General Daniel E. Sickles, and Brigadier General Charles K. Graham in the Trostle House yard in Gettysburg, Pennsylvania.

This is hard for most women, for any woman who would like the full attention, which he did not offer, ever. I believe that he spent so much of his time with the vast camaraderie of men friends and political constituents, that this was his first consideration, and women as equals did not matter as much. They were important, but not the same. They could be soft and loving, which he needed, but when it came down to a real sharing of a common life, they were not the same for Dan.

If it is true that Daniel Sickles apparently spent more time living with Eleanora Wilmerding than any other woman in his life. . . . that must account for something.

Dan continued to work for the Civil War veterans, and for Gettysburg. The battlefields were not taken care of and a lot of businesses were buying up land and the almost hallowed ground was being used not in keeping with the purposes Dan would have liked to see. He attended all of the annual reunions of the blue and gray at Gettysburg and other battlefields, where Union and Confederate troops took part in meeting again, this time in more peaceful surroundings. Even in New York City, he was surrounded by former generals whom he knew, such as General Sherman, who lived on Madison Square, and General Grant, who after completing a world tour with his wife, was considering a run for another term as president in 1880. They met each other many times, planning the strategy.

A turn of events that delighted Dan was a meeting with, of all people, a man also helping to get Grant elected, General James Longstreet.[2] This group really thought that Grant could make the transition back to president, but James Garfield, another Civil War major general, was elected president and in less than a year, on September 19, 1881, became the second sitting president to be the target of an assassin's bullet. General Garfield had been involved in the Western theater of the war, and was also a Congressman before being elected.

In 1881, Dan's father, George G. Sickles, then eighty-one years old, took as his second wife forty-eighty-year-old Mrs. Mary Sheridan Sawyer, a widow with three lovely daughters, names Roma, Althea, called Alta, and Pierie, called Pera, who were of the union of George and Mary.

Mrs. Sickles had been a nurse and housekeeper for some years for the family, and had two sons from her previous marriage, one of whom lived with her before and after the marriage to George Sickles. They lived on Fifth Avenue and North Street in New York City, and on a large farm in New Rochelle, New York. Dan did not attend the wedding, which was a grand social event carried by the local papers. As unconventional as Dan Sickles was himself, he did not allow his own actions over the years to change his attitude towards this marriage. However, his daughter, Laura Carlton, was in attendance, along with Mrs. Antonio Bagioli, her grandmother.

Dan's horror was idleness. He took on the projects of the Presidency of the Society of the Army of the Potomac, and a leader of The Third Army Corps Union. In 1885, Sickles, unhappily, helped bury his old friend, Ulysses Grant, at whose funeral in New York City, he rode at the head of 18,000 Civil War veterans.

George Sickles had just completed a grand marble tomb for himself and his family in Beechwood Cemetery in New Rochelle, when he died. Dan did attend the service and assumed the charges for a dinner for one hundred and fifty friends and family members. His father left a large fortune, mostly composed of property in New York City, and in New Rochelle, New York. With this new inheritance, Dan now had a very personal way to be of benefit to the wanting veterans. This noble cause would continue throughout the remaining active years of his life, making it his first priority.

Today, safe from vandals, who still destroy, and the entrepreneurs striving to commercialize the "Hallowed Ground." This was his life's work now, and he went at it as he had done all of his projects, but this one was not only for himself. . . . .

In the election of 1896 for William McKinley, a group of generals from the Civil War went on a whirlwind speaking tour of the Midwest. Among the group were General Oliver Otis Howard, General Daniel E. Sickles, and General Russell A. Alger. They were Republicans for McKinley. General Howard had lost an arm at Seven Pines in 1862, General Sickles had lost a leg at Gettysburg, and General Alger had been seriously wounded in Boonsboro, Maryland, after the Gettysburg Campaign. The Democrats referred to the three of them as "the Wrecks of the Civil War." I don't think that Dan would have found much humor in that or the name to his liking. Major General Alger fought at Gettysburg, and was before that in the Fifth Michigan, a colonel in the second brigade of George A. Custer's cavalry. He became the governor of Michigan and later in 1897–99, the secretary of war.[3]

By the year 1900, both of Dan's children had visited him in New York City, Stanton even having visited the Chancellorsville area with his father and a group of other officers who saw duty there in 1863.

Stanton had become the youngest attaché in diplomatic circles and had married Comtesse Ysabel Napoleon Magna, daughter of Leonard Brocheton, and Godchild of Queen Mother Isabella. Dan was very proud of his children and enjoyed the pleasure of having them near, as they were his only family, since Laura Buchanan Sickles Carlton had died on December 10, 1891, leaving no children.

Dan headed the New York State Monument Commission for the Battlefield of Gettysburg, and for the next twenty years worked diligently on erecting the monuments and battle position markers in their proper positions in the fields. He would train back and forth between New York and Gettysburg, and return to start all over again. It was a tremendous task and he proved up to the strenuous routine. In between were a few affairs of the heart with ladies, Miss Wilmerding taking notice, but knowing Dan would never change.

Among his papers, this one marked "personal" was a note from a lady as follows . . . and surely kept, out of sentiment . . . "I have just come home, and have your dear note, many many thanks, for it made me very happy to know you still think of me. It is now six o'clock and too late to meet you. It is best, for I might sin. My husband is sitting looking straight at me. Love me still, dear Edgar. It is so sweet to be loved by one so dear, and my sad heart. I am afraid I shall always be so, God forgive me! and bless you for my so dearly loved one."[4]

Around this time, the commanding generals of the Civil War took to writing their autobiographies for posterity, giving their interpretations of the battles they were in during the four years duration of hostilities. In most cases, the enemy was not "the other side" but the generals of their own command who made errors in judgement, as all generals will at one time or another. Dan Sickles was mentioned in a great many of these books as having done the unthinkable in the movement of his saliant, or position, at Gettysburg. Dan was not one to let this "lie" go unnoticed and counteracted by replies to this position in print many times. The years had not dimmed his perception of what he had done, or not done, at all, and his words made some agree, but still most did not, and said so. Generals

Major General Daniel E. Sickles, age 83, at the 1903 reunion of the Battle of Gettysburg.

Longstreet, Alexander, Birney, Hunt, and Warren agreed that the plan was not completely in error and could possibly have been the correct one, had there been more units to back up the action, and sustain the position with help, which did in fact finally arrive.

Dan maintained all the while that his decision helped the Army of the Potomac by tiring out the Confederate troops being thrown by Longstreet. This was true, but the loss of life was immense, and I believe that fact was, hard to say, a success to most commanders. History has shown us that more battles have been lost or gained at heavy cost because the commanders did not know the nature of the ground they were fighting over than any other reason. George Meade, new to command for less than a few days, arriving way after dark, did not know the ground. Gettysburg is such a diversified battlefield that real practical knowledge would have not immediately been applied to such a large number of corps arriving still.

Dan never wrote his story, for whatever reasons he chose. It would have been interesting, to say the least, but perhaps he was correct, for it would have proven too hard a story, too many enemies involved. He did write a long forward to the book about General James Longstreet, which was written by his young widow, after he died, in which Sickles gives detailed events in sequence, but not personal enough. If he had written any thing else, he would have been taken to task for sure.

Dan became involved in doing the correct service to Gettysburg that he was elected to a third term in Congress in 1892–94. This was so he could sponsor a bill making Gettysburg into a National Cemetery where it would always be protected, or hopefully so still. Eda had also married a diplomat, named Dayrell Crackanthorpe, who was

Minister of Great Britain and to many South American legations during his long term in diplomatic positions. Unfortunately, Eda died in 1918 in Nice, France, where she had been a nurse in World War I, and possibly during the worldwide influenza epidemic that killed so many that year, especially in August of 1918. Caroline Sickles decided, with the prodding of her son, Stanton, to reunite his family, after almost three decades of separation, to attempt reconciliation with her husband, if not a true one, at least a softening of attitudes and a face-to-face meeting.

Stanton, now thirty-six years old, had wished for this meeting for many years, visiting his father and taking on himself the position to act as a go-between to his parents. It is assumed that Dan, now eighty-nine years old, was agreeable to the meeting, tense enough though he thought it would be, and mother and son arrived at 23 Fifth Avenue. Their first meeting was pleasant enough and Stanton was elated as he had been working for over six years to reach this point. He was now a father himself and would like nothing more than to see them rejoined at last.

It seemed perfectly logical to Caroline that his housekeeper and friend, Miss Wilmerding's services would no longer be required, and so she would leave and Caroline would move into their home. Caroline could read Eleanora's possessiveness and affection quite readily and her stipulation that if she were to stay, Eleanora or Eleanor, would have to leave. Dan was furious that after twenty-seven years she could return and dictate her terms about himself and Eleanora. No, she would not be dismissed, were his last words!

Unnerved by the reaction, Caroline and Stanton left the house and moved into the Hotel Albert, on Eleventh Street, only a block away from Dan's home. They were halfway to a possible reconciliation, but the chasm made an uneasy truce between them.

Dan Sickles had spent his fortune, but the public still thought of him as a very wealthy man. Many women were still being courted by him, and there was always a supply of jewels and trinkets available in his home for whatever occasion arrived. He did a brisk business with very fashionable New York jewelers.

Caroline and Stanton kept up the idea and hope of permanent reconciliation plans, but the feisty general made a new will, in spite, leaving his entire estate to Eleanora Wilmerding. He had made investments in the stock market, which did not turn out to be real investments at all. The bottomless pit of his resources had hit bottom. He had been enjoying life and its luxuries for too long. He was not meeting his financial obligations and would lose his cherished personal property in the house, unless he could come up with funds to meet the judgments against him.

Caroline, who had stayed for four years close by at the Hotel Albert, heard of this situation and came to his rescue with $8,200 for the judgment, in addition to assuming a second mortgage on his home. She had pawned her own jewelry to pay another $5,050 to bail him out. He was furious about learning this also. She was sorry for his plight, but she would not make herself a pauper any further. She would welcome him with open arms if he wished to make his home with her, but not to save a home where she and the housekeeper would occupy it together.

To make matters worse, a shortage of money had been found in The New York State Monument Commission's books for expenditures for the monuments erected at Gettysburg. Stanton was able to pay $5,000 of the missing funds, about which his father said he knew nothing of how such a shortage could have occurred. Dan was dismissed as head of the commission, and was to be arrested for non-payment of another case, when a friend came on the scene. Some New Yorkers might have been down on General Sickles, but he had one good friend who was distressed by this turn of events, Helen Longstreet, the late general's wife, who telegramed Sickles from Gainesville, Georgia as follows: "My soul is sorrowed by your troubles. Am writing the Attorney General of New York that I will raise money among the ragged destitute, and maimed veterans who followed Lee to pay the amount demanded if New York officials will allow sufficient time. We are writing into our history the story of degenerate descendants of heroic sires. The republic, whose battles you fought, will not permit your degradation."[5]

In July 1913, a grand occasion took place in Dan Sickles's life, the fiftieth anniversary of the Battle of Gettysburg. There would be Dan, one of only four remaining Civil War commanders still living. The other three were General John Rutter Brooke, who was at Gettysburg also with the Second Corps, and later the Military Governor of Cuba and Puerto Rico, and who died on September 5th, 1926. General Joshua Lawrence Chamberlain, Colonel of the Twentieth Maine during the Battle of Gettysburg, died in 1914 from his many war wounds, and General Adelbert Ames, former Colonel of the Twentieth Maine before Chamberlain. Ames died in 1933 at the age of ninety-seven, being the very last Civil War commander to leave this Earth.

Both Dan and Joshua Chamberlain were at Gettysburg before the date of fiftieth anniversary to arrange for the momentous reunion, to involve themselves along with many others going over the details involved in such a large project as this one. Dan was now ninety-three, and could no longer use the crutches as well as before, so his valet friend, Mosely, often pushed him around in a wheelchair,

At his last Gettysburg reunion in 1913, General Sickles is accompanied by Miss Eleanora Earle Wilmerding (right).

although he is pictured as having the crutches as well as being seated in the chair. The Gettysburg Hotel, his usual location for the stay at such affairs, even installed an elevator to accommodate General Sickles, but he wished to stay in one of the tents with friends on the battlefield, to live the life of a soldier one more time. This was to be his last reunion, and I guess it was possible that he expected this would be the last hurrah. . . .

He had however, enjoyed himself sitting on the porch of the Rogers House, directly on Emmitsburg Road and on Pickett's Charge with his friends and cronies, watching the aged veterans of the blue and the gray once more move up the hill, at a slower pace than in 1863 and meet at the walls of The Angle once more, not with guns this time but with handshakes and tears.

Dan and his friend, Twichell, now a young seventy-five-year-old looked again at the monuments together, and his friend remarked that it was a pity that there was no memorial to him. Sickles replied that the whole damned field was his memorial, and so it is. Actually, there are memorials to the man, one a large monument with SICKLES'S EXCELSIOR BRIGADE in huge letters on the top, and upon which in the center between the many columns, was to be placed a bust of Dan Sickles, but it was never placed there, and was last heard of in the studio of the sculptor, wherever that may be.

Another memorial is a bronze plaque stating, "Erected in Compliance With Act of 53rd Congress 3rd Session Introduced By Major General Daniel E. Sickles Representative from 10th District of New York To Establish A Military Park No. Gettysburg Pennsylvania Approved by The President February 11th 1895."

This plaque is on the back of the Abraham Lincoln Memorial in The National Cemetery, and unfortunately it is not read by too many people as they never think to look behind Lincoln's Memorial, where he made his famous address after the Battle of Gettysburg, in November of 1863. Also in his honor there is Sickles Avenue in Gettysburg around the site of The Devil's Den and Little Round Top, and Sickles Road in the location of the Battle of Chancellorsville, Virginia. There is a large granite memorial to the Men of New York, on which are placed the names of men who were at Gettysburg, officers such as Daniel Butterfield, Wesley Merritt, Regis de Trobriand, Thomas Devin Roy Stone, and many dozens more in addition to Daniel E. Sickles. There remains the monument in back of the Trostle barn where Dan's wounding took place, and The Daniel Shaffer Farm, which was also a Third Corps hospital where Dan Sickle's leg was amputated on July 2, 1863, with a plague stating this.

Dan had met his grandson, Daniel Edgar, for a few days in 1910, when Stanton had brought him on a short trip from Europe to New York City. He was a young slender boy of high spirits and his grandfather loved him on sight. Dan wrote a short rather pathetic note to the lad in April 1914.[6]

"My Dear Dan, your old grandpa is ill; he would like to see you once more. I see big clouds in Europe. The Emperor Wilhelm II is a little Bismarck. I predict war, a big war in the near future, but I will not see it. Please ask your mother to send you over to see me." He never did get his wish to see the boy again.

Until recently, Dan had been well and even reported as sprightly on March 29th, 1914. A rumor was spread that he was at the point of death. Late that night, a *New York Times* reporter called up General Sickles's home over the telephone to make inquiry about his condition. The voice at the other end said, "Yes, this is General Sickles. Am I ill? Nonsense, I was never better in my life. There is nothing to that story. It's all a lie!''

The obstacle of reconciliation was removed when for unknown reasons, Eleanora Wilmerding died around April in 1914, with no obituary notice found. Dan must have missed her greatly, as she was a good and loyal friend and companion. Mosely informed Caroline and Stanton of Miss Wilmerding's death and they moved from the hotel where they had been for years into 23 Fifth Avenue, to help care for him and his affairs.

It is written that he did write his memoirs possibly, but that they were stolen, along with his medals, from a safe. He was really alone in his house now, surrounded by ghosts of the past. An unknowing wife and son, thinking of long gone friends, and dreaming of the many women who he had loved, but had never known as well as he could have. Back further to Isabella, and even further back to one who shared the pain of guilt fifty-five years ago in Washington and not spoken of . . . flashing before him were the titles used for him. Congressman, Colonel, Brigadier General, Major General, Military Governor of North and South Carolina, Minister to Spain, holder of both the Congressional Medal of Honor and the French Medal of Honor. A long life passed before his eyes, finally dimming as the evening shadows and flickering lights in the room closed around him and he was off to another realm . . . the legend upheld by him, yet not too far from fact. . . .

So ended the life and times of Daniel Edgar Sickles. A long life filled with adventurous spirit, was what the *New York Times* wrote at his death. He had filled newspapers for sixty-four years, giving his ups and downs, during his life, and he had followed the course, come what may.

Fourteen
Old Soldiers Never Die, but They Do

Daniel Sickles died at 9:10 P.M. on May 3rd, 1914. Caroline and Stanton were by his bedside, with John Kirby, counsel for Mrs. Sickles, and Miss Higgins, a trained nurse. He died just before his doctor, J.H. Spann, arrived. Dr. Spann thought that the attack the old veteran was suffering would prove fatal, on account of his advanced years. The cause of death was a cerebral hemorrhage, followed by a coma of a few days duration.

The body of General Sickles was laid in the parlor of 23 Fifth Avenue, which was banked with flowers, tributes of many friends of the dead soldier. There was a great cross of white roses sent by the State Senate of New York, and a wreath from the New York Assembly. There was also a large triangle of white lilies of the valley that was sent by Harry K. Thaw, who admired General Sickles greatly. Mr. Thaw, as Dan, had been convicted of murder in another sensational trial after the death of the notable architect, Stanford White. Mr. Thaw was also judged not guilty by way of temporary insanity, but was hospitalized for five years in a psychiatric institution in New York. The year was 1913 for his release from Mattewan Asylum for The Criminally Insane. I believe that the triangle shape of the floral arrangement had to do with the involvement of a third party in both affairs and murders.

On top of the coffin was placed the blue and gold cap of the general, his sword, and his golden epaulettes. The coffin was carried from the house and placed on a cassion where the honorary pallbearers formed a line on either side. A Color Sergeant took his stand just behind the cassion carrying the tattered flag from the Battle of Gettysburg. Men of various grand army posts fell in line behind the Philip Kearny men, and the funeral procession closed with members of the general's family. Mrs. Sickles and son, Stanton, in the first carriage, Mrs. Thomas Dunham, sister of the general and her husband, in the second carriage. Others in carriages were General Henry Burnett, Roland Kirby, the architect of many of the monuments on Gettysburg Battlefield, and who had made a death mask of General Sickles. Mrs. Kirby, Mr. and Mrs. Daniel Hays, General James O'Beirne, and several comrades of the Third Army Corps, Prince Pigniatelli, and the Spanish Consul, friend of Mrs. Sickles, and George fry, a former wartime aide of General Sickles.[1]

The onlookers were deeply touched with a sentiment of reverence. The workday thousands lined up along both sides of the sidewalks and were leaning out of the windows of the stores along Fifth Avenue. So they bared their heads as the coffin passed, and told one another in many varieties of English and foreign dialects that it was General Sickles's funeral and that he was a famous warrior.

The bells of Saint Patrick's Cathedral tolled a funeral march as the head of the column came into and on the grounds of the cathedral in view of thousands of people crowded around watching. The mounted police and troops drew up in salute before Saint Patrick's, leaving a clearing for the cortege, which was received at the center aisle. Monsignor Lavalle, after celebrating the High Requiem Mass, delivered the funeral sermon, assisted by three Reverends.

As the coffin was borne out of the cathedral and placed again on the gun caisson, in the street, rain was falling heavily. All of the military escort except the squad of mounted men and the gun squad of the field artillery, drawing the cassion, had disbanded. The aged pallbearers of the Philip Kearny Post, however, did not yield to the cold and heavy downpour and insisted on taking their places in marching order beside the bier. They kept in line all the way down Fifth Avenue to Pennsylvania Station where the body was placed aboard a special train, which at 3:34 P.M. took it and the funeral party to Washington. In Washington, the funeral party was received by a company of regular troops detached by the Secretary of War, Lindley M. Garrison. The coffin was placed under a Guard of Honor in Union Station to remain until the morning.

The next morning, as the procession passed through the grounds of Fort Meyer, a Major General's artillery salute was fired as the body of the veteran corps commander was carried along accompanied by an escort of cavalry and field artillery. At the grave three salvos of rifle shots and another artillery salute marked the placing of the body in its last resting place. In addition to the regular army escort, a very large number of Civil War veterans marched in the procession. A funeral service was read by the Rev. Father J.D. Houlihan, Chaplain of Fort Meyer. So ended the life and times of Daniel Edgar Sickles. A long life filled with, as *The New York Times* noted, "He was truly adventurous spirit." The grand old general was buried and left on the hillside among other fallen comrades to the quietness and the serene beauty of Arlington National Cemetery, the premier military resting place in the United States of America.

Appendix: Tributes, Anecdotes, and Comments on Daniel Edgar Sickles

I here include a group of located articles found pertaining to the life and career of General Daniel Sickles, some little known but nevertheless interesting to those who like more information on this man.

Dan Sickles left few papers about his life. Some were destroyed by a reported fire in his home at 23 Fifth Avenue, New York City. There was also a reported theft at the same location. He chose never to write his autobiography, as most of the Civil War generals did, for whatever reason he judged advantageous. Perhaps he himself was too controversial a person to write about himself. The newspapers provided a wealth of information, but not always accurate or complimentary.

Many books have short references to Sickles of little known facts about him and many repeat the usual one sentence or paragraph about the foolhardy move at Gettysburg, not investigating the long road of trying to get attention from the commanding general, George G. Meade about the merits involved in Sickles's plan. I believe that the great loss of life on July 2, 1863 hurt his aura more than anything else. One has to do a lot of searching to find the man. What are the most interesting are the bits of information that are found in records of conversation and stories of people involved with Dan Sickles.

He outlived all of his contemporaries, the only still surviving in 1914 being General Albert Ames, former commander of the Twentieth Maine, before Colonel Joshua Lawrence Chamberlain took over the leadership a few days before that fateful summer day in 1863.

Major General Daniel Sickles was one of both Federal and Confederate Generals who visited Gettysburg in 1893 for a reunion, and were escorted by a professional guide, Captain Jesse Bowman Young, who lived in or near Gettysburg and had studied the battle intensively. They all stood on "Little Round Top" and listened while he explained everything that happened then, and even though they had all been there in July of 1863, in the heat of battle, they were given an over-view that gave details that even they as combatants could not have known about, the larger scope of the entire battle, and they appreciated hearing the wider story. Both Dan Sickles and James Longstreet had been up on "Little Round Top" together, remembering when they were opponents in the life and death struggle. The less active Longstreet, depending on his friend's one-legged aid, chuckling, "Yes sir, you ought to be helping me, seeing the way you kept me from getting up here in '63!"[1]

One likes to think of those two in their sturdy gnarled seventies, as contemporaries reported them, as guests of honor at a banquet in Charleston, the deaf Longstreet leaning on the shoulder of the crippled Sickles, the better to hear his after dinner speech, then himself singing in good voice, the "Star Spangled Banner" after the Saint Patrick's Day celebration in Atlanta. Both somewhat mellowed, alternately seeing each other home. Longstreet insisted at the door of his hotel, "Sickles, you are a cripple and I cannot leave you on these dark streets alone. I shall go back with you." And with a few nips of Irish whiskey at each end to sustain them. Sickles insisted, "Old fellow, you are deaf and you might get run over by a hack. I shall go back with you." They wove their way along the rickety board sidewalk, arm in arm gossiping about the past.

They met again in March 1901, at a reception given to President McKinley on his second inauguration. In the midst of the great throng assembled on that occasion, he and Longstreet had quite a reception of their own. He was accompanied by his wife, Mrs. Longstreet, named Helen. Everyone admired the blended courtliness and gallantry of the veteran hero towards the ladies who were presented to him and his charming wife.

Sickles and Longstreet met again at West Point for a Centennial and they sat together on the dias, near President Theodore Roosevelt, the Secretary of War, Mr. Root, and the commander of the army, Lieutenant General Miles. Here among his fellow graduates of the Military Academy, Longstreet received a great ovation from the vast audience that filled Column Hall. Again and again he was cheered, when he turned to Sickles exclaiming, "Sickles, what are they cheering about?" "They are cheering you, General" was Sickles's reply. Joy lighted up Longstreet's countenance, the war was forgotten, and he was at home once more at West Point. . . .

Again Sickles and Longstreet stood upon the same platform, in Washington on May 30, 1902 on Memorial Day. Together they reviewed with President Roosevelt, the magnificent column of Union veterans that marched past the President's reviewing stand. That evening, General Longstreet joined General Sickles in visiting to the thousand or more soldiers of the Third Army Corps, assembled in a tent near the White House. These veterans, with a multitude of their comrades, had come to Washington to commemorate another Memorial Day in the Capitol of the nation. The welcome given to General Longstreet by this crowd of old soldiers, who had fought him with all of their might again and again, on so many battlefields could hardly have been more cordial if he had found himself in the midst of an equal number of his own command.

His speech to the men was felicitous and enthusiastically cheered. He said, "I hope to live long enough to see my surviving comrades march side by side with the Union veterans along Pennsylvania Avenue, and then I will die."

This was the last time that the two old Civil War commanders would ever meet again. . . . Sickles commented, "Farewell, Longstreet! I shall follow you very soon. May we meet in a happy realm where strife is unknown and friendship is eternal."

There is a notarized document signed by Daniel Sickles stating that his wife and son, Stanton were visitors in Madrid 1881–1889 when Stanton came to the United States and joined Dan and lived with him until May of 1897, when Stanton entered the diplomatic service of the United States. He would have been about nine years old when his father left Europe in 1881. In 1889 he would have been seventeen, and in 1897 he would have reached about twenty-five years of age.

There is a photograph, undated, but perhaps about 1893, showing a group of men, eight in number, who are standing in front of Chancellorsville House in Virginia, including The Compte of Paris, Daniel Sickles, his son, Stanton, who looks to be a young man of eighteen or twenty years old, who resembles his mother greatly, but there is a resemblance to his father also. I have never read of any account of their living together for so long a period, but they must have seen each other occasionally over the years.

The Old Excelsior Brigade's Chaplain, Reverend Joseph Twichell's best friend was the writer Mark Twain, who had heard his friend speak about Daniel Sickles with love and respect, and when the two finally met in New York City, where Twain had moved very close to Dan's home at 23 Fifth Avenue, they shared many a talk about the war. Twain liked to hear him tell of the events and personalities he encountered. Dan did so with dignity and some benign criticism at that point in his life.

In October 1897, the Secretary of War directed that a Medal of Honor to Major General Daniel E. Sickles, U.S. Volunteers, the medal to be engraved as follows: "The Congress to Major Gen. Daniel E. Sickles for gallantry at Gettysburg, Pa., July 2, 1863."[2] When news of this issuing of the medal became known to Dan, he must have been overcome with joy and deeply proud. He wished to have it gold plated, which was done later.

Brigadier General Henry Tremain, Sickles's friend and aide de camp for many years, worked diligently in trying to obtain a like medal for the Battle of Chancellorsville when Dan had worked against Stonewall Jackson, but the plan was turned down as Dan had done nothing more than his "duty" as was determined. Tremain also was instrumental in trying to get Dan moved into being a Lieutenant General, but that plan did not get approved either.

Daniel Sickles was honored by a memorandum for the Army Register of 1898, with the following statement: "Sickles, Daniel E. Major General, retired, for most distinguished gallantry in action at Gettysburg, Pa., July 2, 1863, displaying on the field both before and after the loss of his leg; while serving as Major General of Volunteers, Commanding the Third Army Corps." Dan was moved by this award, a tribute to his valor and dedication that was appreciated by him.

A verse written by a friend, Horatio King . . . general USA

I see him on that famous field
The bravest of the brave,
Where Longstreet's legions strove to drive
The Third Corps to its grave.

The fight was bloody, fierce, and long
And Sickles's name shall stay
Forever in the Hall of Fame
As he who saved the day.[3]

Colonel Phillip R. de Trobriand, Third Brigade, First Division, Third Corps, made this comment about Dan Sickles:

> Sickles was one of the striking figures of this war. More as a man than a general; in many ways a typical American. He was gifted in high degree with that multiplicity of faculties, which have given rise to the saying that a Yankee is ready for anything.
>
> He has quick perception, an energetic will, prompt and supple intelligence, an active temperament. Naturally ambitious, he brings to the service of his ambitions a clear view, a practical judgment, and a deep knowledge of political tactics. When he has determined on anything, he prepares the way, assembles his forces, and marches directly to the assault. Obstacles do not discourage him, he has many strings on his bow; if he breaks one, he will replace it with another. In him, ability does not exclude frankness. He likes, on the contrary, to play with the cards on the table with his friends and against his enemies. . . .[4]
>
> These three paragraphs sum up Daniel Sickles as well as anything ever written. . . .

It is interesting to note that a letter from the War Department, Office of the Quartermaster General, about the future cortege of General Sickles was signed by Colonel

John L. Clem, who was the "Johnny Clem, the Drummer Boy of Chickamauga," and also called Johnny Shiloh. His name was John Joseph Klem, but when he joined the Twenty-second Mass, as a mascot and drummer boy as a young lad, he changed his name to John Lincoln Clem. He later became a Brigadier General. He was the last Civil War veteran on the Army rolls at the time of his retirement in 1915. He died at the age of eighty-five in San Antonio, Texas, and was buried at Arlington Cemetery in Virginia.

It has been recorded in official United States legal documents that General Sickles was to be buried at Gettysburg after his death. That he requested of his wife just before his death that he wished to be buried in Gettysburg, near the New York Monument in the National Cemetery. A telegram exists stating that this would be allowed, but he was buried in Arlington National Cemetery, which is considered the premier military cemetery in the United States. His spirit resides where ever he wishes it to be. . . .

Daniel E. Sickles took an unmissed opportunity with great personal risk, which still remains to this day, a controversial topic by anyone who has studied the second day of the Battle of Gettysburg, July 2, 1863. There was no personal glory to be gained, just endeavoring to do the best with troops and the terrain that was to be fought upon.

During the Sickles residence in Livingston, city people at heart, the family in time returned to New York; some alien faces, strange visitors, were seen in the old road destined to become Beaufort Avenue. The members of the Sickles family were ever mixed up with all kinds of people, artistic, colorful, and exotic. Musicians and poets abounded among them. There was, for example, the Da Ponte family. The elder Lorenzo Da Ponte, though an old man, doubtless journeyed out of New York to visit his friends in Livingston. Vivid, with a brilliant if lurid past. Years before in

Farmhouse of George G. Sickles on Beaufort Avenue in Livingston, New Jersey. The house was built between 1800 and 1820, and is shown here in 1996. (Photo by Jeanne W. Knoop)

Prague, he had been a close friend of Mozart and had written the lyrics for the composer's famous operas, *The Marriage of Figaro,* and *Don Giovanni.*

In the old days, Da Ponte had been a boon companion of Casanova, a great lover long before John Barrymore. Da Ponte's son Charles, was a professor at Columbia and New York Universities and became an intimate friend of young Dan Sickles. It was into this Bohemian family that the future general eventually married. His bride was Teresa Bagioli, daughter of the ward of the elder Da Ponte.

It was probably due to the Da Pontes that the Sickles family came to Livingston to live. Isaac Samo, who was running the inn at Livingston Center when it was the place of the township's first town meeting, did not remain here long. A well-known musician, having been the orchestra leader in the Park Theater in Park Row, New York, he eventually returned to the life he loved. He moved in professional circles, and it is entirely likely that he knew the Da Pontes and often spoke of them of his sojourn in the pleasant little town in New Jersey. The Da Pontes in turn, mentioned Livingston to their friends, the Sickles.[5]

Why do I question the artificial leg that was made for Dan Sickles not being used, at least in photographs? It seems almost unbelievable that this was so all through the remainder of his life. I have never seen as yet, a standing photograph of the general as he stood after the loss of his leg.

I realize that artificial limbs are far superior today as to mobility and lightness of weight than in the Civil War years. He wrote in letters that he had waited until the stump had healed enough to be fitted, obtained the limb, practiced walking, had perfected its use, and was ready to resume the command of his old Third Corps. He did state that the artificial leg was capricious and he preferred to use the crutches, and moved about quicker and better than the usual user for fifty years. Why would an always fastidious and in-constant-motion man choose not to be seen as he once was and could be again, with the trousers covering the artificial leg? He had never given up before!

It had been stated many times in print that this use of crutches was his way of accepting his wounding that would be visible to all who saw him, a battle, "a Red Badge of Courage." If I know of this man as well as I think, that is probably true. I do not believe that he put himself through such discomfort to accept pity for himself. He was not that kind of man, and never would be.

One contribution that there can be no controversy over is the realization that Dan Sickles deserves nothing but esteem from the entire country for the establishment of Gettysburg National Park as a memorial as it stands today. He led the way to erect monuments to all of the New York troops who fought there, and went on to be elected to a third time as a member of the House of Representatives to rescue the fought-for land from vandals and souvenir hunters. He did not cease battling for the grounds of Gettysburg when he was carried off the field the evening of July 2, 1863. Also in the bill was a provision for acquiring lands to those already donated by other organizations. Congress defined the park as those lands, "occupied by the infantry, cavalry, and artillery on the first, second, and third day of July, eighteen hundred and sixty-three, and such adjacent lands . . . deemed necessary to preserve the important topographical features of the battlefields."[6]

It was not until 1990, however, that congress enacted a bill putting official boundaries on Dan Sickles's hand-drawn sketch of what he envisioned as the battlefield area belonging to all Americans. The 1990 "boundary law" created a park encompassing 5,733 acres, one hundred fourteen privately owned tracts, totaling 1,695 acres, and 55 acres of land owned by the county government lie within today's boundary. It is these acres that must be preserved for future generations through the purchase of their development of full ownership rights. This many persons today are striving to accomplish, before any more land is totally gone that belongs to all Americans.

General Sickles died in New York in 1914, at age ninety-four. A year before his death, the sturdy old man came to my parents' home in Livingston, I believe, in a carriage drawn by a team of horses, and asked my father to go with him to the house on Beaufort Avenue. He was not quite sure of the way, he said, it had been so long ago. Of course my father went, and the old general had his last look at the home in which he had lived as a boy. Seventy-six years had gone by since the bright summer morning when the determined youth had walked away on the path of adventure. (From "Flames Above The Riker," *Vignettes of Old Livingston*, by Freeman Harrison, 1965)

George Garrett Sickles owned two cemetery locations for his two families, Greenwood Cemetery in Brooklyn, New York, and Beechwood Cemetery in New Rochelle, New York, where his second family is buried. The members are at this location, George G. Sickles, his second wife, Mary Sheridan Sawyer Sickles, and their three daughters, Roma, Althea, and Perie.

Endnotes

Chapter One
July 2, 1863, The Day the World Changed

1. *The Civil War, Illustrated History,* p. 224, by Geoffrey Ward, Ric & Ken Burns.
2. *Gettysburg, The Second Day,* p. 333–334, by Harry Pfanz.
3. Sickles's own statement of August 1882.
4. *Lincoln and Sickles,* by Lt. Col. James F. Rusling, by the Third Corps Union, 1910.
5. Contents of original letter by Daniel E. Sickles about the placing of the tanbark.
6. *Lincoln and Sickles,* by the Third Corps Union 1910, by Rusling.
7. *The New York Times* of September 9, 1863.
8. *Sickles the Incredible,* W. A. Swanberg, p. 233–234

Chapter Two
Searching for an Education

1. From The Personal Memoirs of Edwin A. Ely, p. 330.
   Ruth L. Lockwood Memorial Library at The Public Library of Livingston, New Jersey.
2. Harper's Weekly of April 9, 1863. A front page story of Sickles's early career life in Princeton, New Jersey.
3. Map of Livingston area of Essex County, New Jersey, 1859 Livingston Historical Society, Livingston, New Jersey.
4. From Fire Above The Riker; Vignettes of Old Livingston, by Freeman Harrison, 1965, Ruth L. Lockwood Memorial Library at The Public Library of Livingston, New Jersey.

Chapter Three
Growing Up with Teresa

1. *New York Herald,* of March 2, 1853. Both marriage dates released on March 2, 1853. The first on September 27, 1852 was released later. The first civil ceremony, the later a Catholic ceremony.

Chapter Four
Tammany Life; Fast and Loose

1. *New York World*, June 30, 1869.
2. *Sickles's Papers*, Library of Congress, after 1900.

Chapter Five
The Secretary of the American Legation

1. *Harper's Weekly*, April 9, 1859.
2. *The New York World*, June 30, 1869.
3. *Sickles the Incredible*, p. 54.

Chapter Six
New York's Newest Congressman in Washington

1. Stockton Mansion rented in the fall of 1857. Known previously as the Levi Woodbury House and several names in addition. *The Congressman Who Got Away with Murder*, pages 63–64, Brant.
2. *New York Times*, March 15, 1859. The baptism was supposed to take place on Sunday March 14, 1858.

Chapter Seven
A Tragedy for All Concerned

1. *A Belle of the Fifties*, p. 98.
2. *Trial of Daniel Sickles*, p. 72. The identity of the writer was never known, but the handwriting was judged to possibly be a woman's.
3. *The Washington Evening Star*, February 28, 1859.
4. *Trial of Daniel Sickles*, p. 75.
5. *Trial of Daniel Sickles*, p. 42–43.
6. Ibid., p. 7
7. *Sickles the Incredible*, p. 62.
8. *Dan Sickles, Hero of Gettysburg and Yankee King of Spain*, p. 134–135.
9. Ibid., p. 60.
10. *Dan Sickles, Hero of Gettysburg and Yankee King of Spain*, p. 70.
11. Ibid., p. 71.

Chapter Eight
Hunkered Down in Congress; the Lowest Point

1. *Harper's Weekly*, May 14, 1859.
2. *New York Herald*, July 19, 1859.
3. Ibid.
4. *Harper's Weekly*, July 17, 1859.

Chapter Nine
Duty, Honor, and Country

1. *Journal of the Military Service of the US Vol.* Vol. V., #22 p. 151.
2. *Sickles's Papers,* New York Library, October 27, 1861
3. *Four Years with the Army of the Potomac,* by Philippe Regis de Trobriand, p. 425
4. *New York Tribune,* July 22, 1861. The Excelsior Brigade was moved south soon after the disastrous Battle of Bull Run.

Chapter Ten
The Years of War

1. *Harper's Weekly,* June 21, 1862.
2. *Sickles's the Incredible,* p. 157.
3. Ibid., p. 143.
4. Ibid., p. 173.
5. *Dan Sickles,* p. 165.
6. *Sickles the Incredible,* p. 193.
7. *Sickles the Incredible,* p. 197.
8. *The Life of David Bell Birney,* 1867, reprinted 1987.

Chapter Eleven
Rebuilding the Union; the Reconstruction Period

1. Telegram from Abraham Lincoln to Daniel E. Sickles of January 29, 1864 John G. Nicolay and John Hay, *Complete Works of Abraham Lincoln,* 12 volumes, 1894.
2. Telegram from President Lincoln to Daniel E. Sickles of February 10, 1864, from the same source.
3. *The Rough Side of War,* by Chesley A. Mosman 1987.
4. Copy of death certificate of Teresa Bagioli Sickles, dated February 5, 1867.
5. *Dan Sickles,* by Edgecomb Pinchon, p. 225.
6. *The New York Times* of March 7, 1869.

Chapter Twelve
Isabella and Paris

1. Daniel E. Sickles's letters, to Charles K. Graham, dated October 27, 1870.
2. "Letter of John Hay, Secretary of the American Legation in Madrid to Robert Lincoln," the President's son, dated May 7, 1870.
3. *Sickles the Incredible,* p. 331.

4. Ibid., p. 356.

Chapter Thirteen
Home Again and Back to Congress: First Priority, Gettysburg

1. *The Writings of Mark Twain,* his autobiography, p. 337–342.
2. *The New York Times* of May 31, 1880.
3. Autobiography of General Oliver Otis Howard, p. 369.
4. *Daniel E. Sickles's Papers,* New York Public Library, New York.
5. *The New York Times* of January 28, 1914.
6. *Daniel E. Sickles's Papers,* New York Public Library, letter to grandson, dated April 1914.

Chapter Fourteen
Old Soldiers Never Die, but They Do

1. *New York Times,* May 4, 1914.

Appendix: Tributes, Anecdotes, and Comments on Daniel Edgar Sickles

1. *Men and Memories,* by John Russell, New York: 1901.
2. Two bills to authorize the President of the United States to appoint Major General Daniel E. Sickles, retired, to be a lieutenant general of the United States Army, dated December 6, 1909, and February 9, 1912.
3. Tribute written by General Horatio King at the Third Corps Union banquet, May 9, 1908.
4. De Trobriand's comment about General Sickles, from *Four Years With the Army of the Potomac,* by Regis de Trobriand, Boston: 1889, p. 398.
5. *Flames Above the Riker: Vignettes of Old Livingston,* by Freeman Harrison, 1965.
6. Gettysburg National Park, established as a Federal Park, February 11, 1895.

Bibliography

Adams, George W. *Doctors in Blue: The Medical History of the Union Army in the Civil War.* New York: 1952.

Alexander, Edward Porter. *Fighting for the Confederacy.* Dayton, Ohio: Morningside House, 1989.

Arrington, B.T. *The Medal of Honor at Gettysburg.* Gettysburg, Pa: Thomas Publications, 1996.

Biglow, John Jr., *The Campaign of Chancellorsville.* New Haven: 1910.

Brandt, Nat. *The Congressman Who Got Away with Murder.* Syracuse: Syracuse University Press, 1991.

Brown, Henry Lefeure. *A History of the Third Regiment: Sickle's Excelsior Brigade.* Jamestown, New York: 1902.

Brown, Kent Masterson. *Cushing at Gettysburg.* The University Press of Kentucky, 1993.

Busey, John W., and Kathleen R. George. *Nothing but Glory.*

Clemens, Samuel Langhorne. *Mark Twain's Autobiography.* New York: 1924.

Coco, Gregory. *A Strange and Blighted Land.* Gettysburg, PA: Thomas Publications, 1994.

———. *Field Hospitals at Gettysburg, Listed and Photographed July 4–Nov. 20, 1863.* Gettysburg, PA: Thomas Publications, 1988.

Connelly, Thomas and Barbara Bellows. *God and General Longstreet.* 1982.

Davis, O.W. *The Life of David Bell Birney.* 1987.

Doubleday, Abner. *Chancellorsville and Gettysburg.* New York: 1882.

Fontaine, Felix G. *The Washington Tragedy: Trial of Daniel Sickles.* 1859.

Frassanito, William A., *Gettysburg, A Journey in Time,* 1973.

Gramm, Kent. *Gettysburg, A Meditation on War and Values,* Indiana University Press, 1994.

Grant, Ulysses S. *Personal Memoirs,* 2 vols. New York: 1885.

Hassler, William Woods. *A.P. Hill: Lee's Forgotten General.* Chapel Hill: University of North Carolina Press, 1962.

Herbert, Walter H. *Fighting Joe Hooker.* Indianapolis: 1944.

Howard, Oliver Otis. *Autobiography of Oliver Otis Howard,* 2 vols. New York: 1907.

Lincoln, Abraham. *The Complete Works of Abraham Lincoln,* 12 vols. Edited by John G. Nicholay and John Hay. New York: 1894.
Longacre, Edward G. *The Cavalry at Gettysburg.* Associated University Press, 1993.
Longstreet, Helen D. *Lee and Longstreet at High Tide.* With introduction by General Daniel E. Sickles, Gainesville, GA: 1989.
Lyons, J.B., New York Monument Committee. *Final Report of the Battle of Gettysburg,* vols. I, II, III, 1902.
Magner, Blake A. *Traveller and Company: The Horses of Gettysburg,* Gettysburg, PA: Farnsworth House, 1995.
Meade, George. *The Life and Letters of General George Gordon Meade,* vol. 2, New York: 1913.
Naisawald, L. Van Loan, *Grape and Canister: Story of the Field Artillery of the Army of the Potomac,* 1861–1865, 1960.
Nevins, Allen. *The War for the Union. New York: Scribner, 1959.*
Nicholay, John G., and John Hay. *Abraham Lincoln, a History,* vol. 10, 1904.
Nolan, Alan T. *The Iron Brigade.* New York: Macmillan, 1971.
O'Toole, Patricia. *The Five of Hearts.* 1990.
Pfanz, Harry W. *Gettysburg, Culp's Hill and Cemetery Hill.* 1993.
———. *Gettysburg, the Second Day.* Chapel Hill and London: University of North Carolina Press, 1987.
Pinchon, Edgecomb. *Dan Sickles, Hero of Gettysburg, "Yankee King of Spain."* New York: Doubleday Doran & Co., 1945.
Ray, William Stanley. *Gettysburg Reunion of 1913.* PA: 50th State Printers, 1914.
Revere, Joseph Warren. *Keel and Saddle.* 1872.
Russo, Joseph L. *Lorenzo Da Ponte, Poet and Adventurer.* New York: 1922.
Rusling, James F. *Men and Things I Saw in Civil War Days.* New York: 1899.
Shreve, Major William P. *The Story of the Third Army Corps Union.* Boston: 1910.
Sterling, Ada A. *Belle of the Fifties: The Memoirs of Mrs. Clay of Alabama.* Doubleday, Page and Co., New York: 1905.
Swanberg, W.A. *Sickles the Incredible.* New York: Charles Scribner and Sons, 1956.
Tremain, Henry F. *Two Days of War.* 1905.
Ward, Geoffrey, and Ken and Richard Burns. *Civil War Illustrated History.* New York: Alfred A. Knopf, Inc., 1990.
Washington, John E. *They Knew Lincoln.* E.P. Dutton and Co., New York: 1942.
Wert, Jeffrey D. *General James Longstreet.* New York: Simon and Schuster, 1993.
Williams, Kenneth P. *Lincoln Finds a General.* vol. 11. 1941.
Williams, Harry T. *Lincoln and His Generals.*

Booklets

Rusling, General James. *Lincoln and Sickles.* Third Corps Union, 1910.

Printed Documents

Historical Survey of Lafayette Square. Washington, D.C.: John Carl Warnecke and Associates, 1967.

Periodicals and Newspapers

Harper's Weekly, 1859
The New York Times, 1859, 1900, 1914
The New York Tribune, 1867, 1890, 1904, 1910
Washington Star, 1865–67

Maps

Essex County, New Jersey, 1859
Essex County, New Jersey, 1906

Articles

Longacre, Edward.
"Damnable Dan Sickles, He Lusted for Love and Battle." *Civil War Times Illustrated*, 23, no. 3, (May 1984): 16–25.

Heming, Thomas J. "A Husband's Revenge." *American Heritage*, April 1969, p. 65–75.

Balderson, Thomas. "The Sad, Shattered Life of Teresa Sickles." *American Heritage Illustrated* 17, no. 5, (September 1982): 41–45.

Index